A TO Z GREAT FILM DIRECTORS

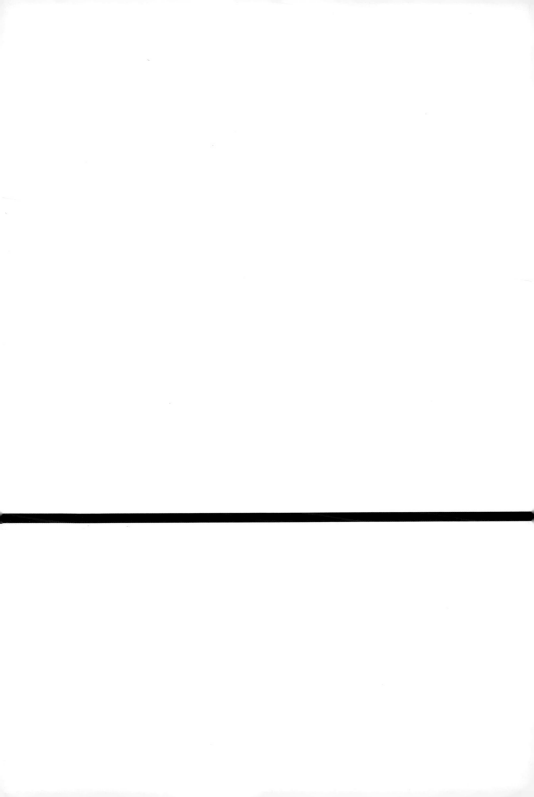

# A TO Z GREAT FILM DIRECTORS
# ANDY TUOHY

## WITH TEXT BY MATT GLASBY

CASSELL
ILLUSTRATED

An Hachette UK Company
www.hachette.co.uk

First published in Great Britain in 2015 by Cassell,
an imprint of Octopus Publishing Group Ltd
Carmelite House
50 Victoria Embankment
London EC4Y 0DZ
www.octopusbooks.co.uk
www.octopusbooksusa.com

This edition published in 2018

Distributed in the US by Hachette Book Group
1290 Avenue of the Americas, 4th and 5th Floors
New York, NY 10104

Distributed in Canada by Canadian Manda Group
664 Annette St., Toronto, Ontario, Canada M6S 2C8

ISBN 978 1 78840 056 5

A CIP catalogue record for this book is available from the British Library

Printed and bound in China

10 9 8 7 6 5 4 3 2 1

# CONTENTS

# PREFACE

Creating an *A to Z of Great Directors* was always going to be fraught with danger, not least the restrictive format – how on earth do you edit 125 years of cinematic history into 52 names? Beyond the obvious 'big hitters', whom few people would argue against: Hitchcock, Kubrick, Lean, Scorsese, I wasn't sure where to start. So on suggestion of the estimable Matt Glasby we instigated the five films rule as a barometer of greatness. And this is where the trouble really began; I soon realized one man's *Last Temptation of Christ* is another's *Last Airbender*. Then there are anomalies like Orson Welles, who wrote, directed and produced the classic *Citizen Kane*, then never made another of such irrefutable importance.

When you stack up the odds against any film coming into existence it's a miracle they happen at all: good, bad or indifferent. So to create even one or two works that have left a lasting cinematic legacy should be applauded, loudly. And, of course, there are plenty of great directors who didn't make the cut but I would have liked to have included – one of my all-time favourites, Jacques Tati, being a good example. He was up against stiff competition in the Ts, though, with Tarantino and Truffaut.

We have tried to shine a light on a range of international directors, some better known in their own countries than globally. Indeed, were it not for the research that went into this book I might never have been enlightened by the charms of Japan's Yasujirō Ozu or India's Satyajit Ray, and I can now count Ozu, belatedly, as one of my favourites. And we also wanted to ensure that often-overlooked female directors were properly represented too. The comparatively small number in the book is reflective of the industry, and there are many up-and-coming female directors such as Ava DuVernay who will undoubtedly be on the list of greats before long.

You may also notice that some letters have been omitted because we wanted to avoid shoe-horning in directors just for the sake of it. After all, what's a Q between friends?

*Andy Tudor*

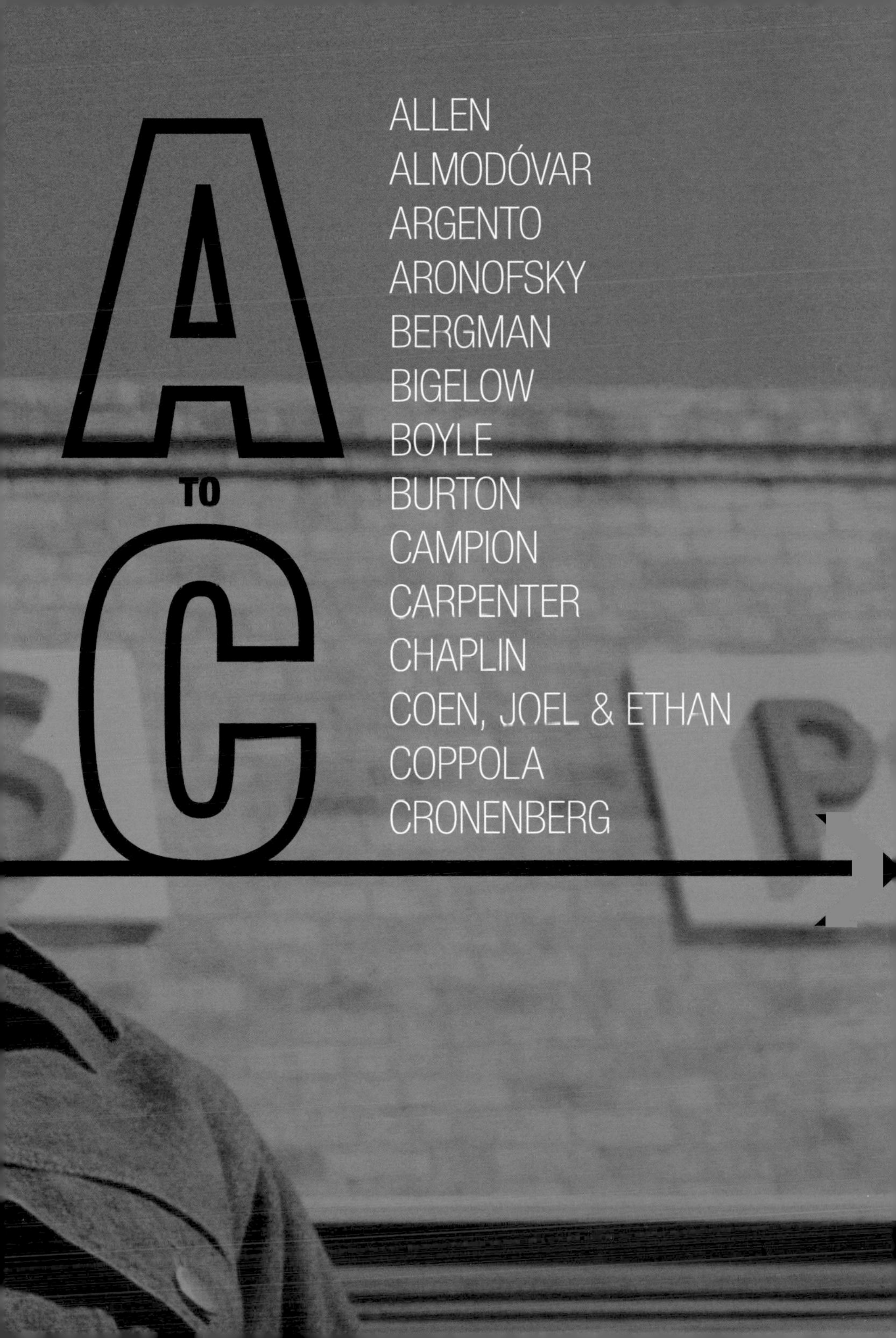

# A to C

ALLEN
ALMODÓVAR
ARGENTO
ARONOFSKY
BERGMAN
BIGELOW
BOYLE
BURTON
CAMPION
CARPENTER
CHAPLIN
COEN, JOEL & ETHAN
COPPOLA
CRONENBERG

# WOODY
# ALLEN

AMERICAN
BORN 1935

There is prolific, then there is the man born Allan Stewart Konigsberg. The writer, director and (often) star of his own comedy-dramas, this neurotic New Yorker has made around one film a year since 1965. After an unhappy childhood in Brooklyn, Allen became a TV gag writer, stand-up comic and playwright, mining the embarrassments of his early years for his self-lacerating monologues. Unhappy with what became of his first script, *What's New Pussycat?* (1965), he turned director for the likes of *What's Up, Tiger Lily?* (1966) and *Sleeper* (1973), which he would later call his 'early, funny films'.

With *Annie Hall* (1977), a New York tale of soul-searching and lost love, Allen paved the way for modern rom-coms such as *When Harry Met Sally...* (1989), pre-empted TV's *Friends* (1994–2004) and won all of the main five Oscars, except Best Actor. In it, stand-up comic Alvy Singer (Allen) whizzes us through his relationship with Annie (Diane Keaton), forever breaking the fourth wall to petition the audience directly. One scene has Alvy and Annie awkwardly flirting while subtitles tell us what they are really thinking. If only they could read each other properly, you feel, Allen's work would be done. The battle between the sexes continues in *Manhattan* (1979), a black-and-white ode to Allen's home town and younger women. The latter aspect would prove uncomfortably autobiographical when Allen left girlfriend Mia Farrow for her adopted teenage daughter Soon-Yi Previn.

## FILMS TO SEE
★ *Sleeper* (1973)
★ *Annie Hall* (1977)
★ *Manhattan* (1979)
★ *Hannah and Her Sisters* (1986)
★ *Blue Jasmine* (2013)

## DID YOU KNOW?
After 40 years in therapy, Allen told the *New York Times*: 'People always tease me. They say, look at you, you went for so much psychoanalysis and you're so neurotic... [But] I'm not sure I could have done all of that without being in psychoanalysis.'

Hey, don't knock masturbation!
It's sex with someone I love.

 *ANNIE HALL*

During the 1980s and 1990s Allen's films riffed, referenced and borrowed like his beloved jazz music. *Stardust Memories* (1980) is based on Federico Fellini's *8½* (1963), while *Hannah and Her Sisters* (1986) nods to Ingmar Bergman, and many of his works dipped into the darker territory of *Husbands and Wives* (1992). After acclaimed comedies such as

*Annie Hall*, 1977

*Bullets over Broadway* (1994) and *Sweet and Lowdown* (1999), Allen decamped to London for *Match Point* (2005), then continental Europe for *Vicky Cristina Barcelona* (2008) and *Midnight in Paris* (2011). His muse revived, he returned to the United States for the critically lauded *Blue Jasmine* (2013). Set under a weak San Francisco sun, it starred Cate Blanchett as – guess what? – a neurotic New Yorker. ★

*Manhattan*, 1979

WOODY ALLEN'S

MANHATTAN

# PEDRO
# ALMODÓVAR

SPANISH
BORN 1949

The phrase 'un film de Almodóvar' is much more than a guarantee of quality. Spain's best-loved writer-director, the most successful name in LGBT-friendly cinema, has won international prizes aplenty (Oscars, Cannes awards and Goyas – the Spanish Oscars), and made stars of Penélope Cruz and Antonio Banderas, but the real draw is the way his films speak for people of all kinds, irrespective of their persuasions.

Pedro Almodóvar Caballero was born in rural Calzada de Calatrava during the repressive Franco era. In keeping with the generosity of spirit exhibited in his films, his father was a winemaker and his mother transcribed letters for the illiterate. Religious boarding school beckoned, but, 'Cinema became my real education, much more than the one I received from the priest,' he told writer Marvin D'Lugo. He moved to Madrid to study film, deciding to teach himself when Franco closed the National School of Cinema. Franco's death in 1975 led to a transgressive cultural renaissance, with Almodóvar at the forefront. Flirtations with experimental theatre, glam rock and short films made way for features, the first of which was the flawed but fondly remembered *Pepi, Luci, Bom* (1980).

Since then, 'un film de Almodóvar' has come to mean compassionate, blackly comic melodramas such as *Women on the Verge of a Nervous Breakdown* (1988), *Tie Me Up! Tie Me Down!* (1990) and *Volver* (2006). Though mistrustful of the state (*Live*

## FILMS TO SEE
★ *Women on the Verge of a Nervous Breakdown* (1988)
★ *All about My Mother* (1999)
★ *Bad Education* (2004)
★ *Volver* (2006)
★ *The Skin I Live In* (2011)

## DID YOU KNOW?
Almodóvar showed his raunchy early Super 8 films, including *The Fall of Sodom* (1975) and *Fuck Me, Fuck Me, Fuck Me, Tim* (1978), in bars. Because they had no soundtracks, he performed all the dialogue and singing himself.

EL DESEO PRÉSENTE UN FILM DE

# ALMODÖVAR

# VOLVER

PENÉLOPE CRUZ         CARMEN MAURA         LOLA DUEÑAS
BLANCA PORTILLO       YOHANA COBO      ET CHUS LAMPREAVE

DIRECTEUR DE LA PHOTOGRAPHIE JOSÉ LUIS ALCAINE       MONTAGE JOSÉ SALCEDO       MUSIQUE ALBERTO IGLESIAS
PRODUCTEUR EXÉCUTIF AGUSTÍN ALMODÓVAR          PRODUIT PAR ESTHER GARCÍA

ÉCRIT ET RÉALISÉ PAR PEDRO ALMODÓVAR

france inter          CANAL+          WWW.VOLVER-LEFILM.COM          PATHÉ

Volver, 2006

> Cinema can fill in the empty
> spaces of your life and your
> loneliness.

 PEDRO ALMODÓVAR

*Flesh*, 1997) and the ▮
2004), they are admiri▮
in all its forms, and ac▮
kinds. *All about My M*▮
transsexual prostitute▮
lesbian actress; *Talk t*▮
matador. Indeed, strong female characters
appear throughout his work. 'Women are more
spectacular as dramatic subjects,' he told the authors of *Almodóvar secreto*, 'they
have a greater range of registers.'

Over the years Almodóvar's own registers have shifted, too – into horror, for surgery-
themed *The Skin I Live In* (2011), and the highest of high camp, for the airplane-set *I'm
So Excited* (2013) – while still giving voice to outsiders everywhere. ★

*Bad Education*, 2004

To experience a film by the Italian horror maestro Dario Argento is to immerse yourself, willingly, in a bad dream. Illogic reigns, swollen colours and sounds swamp the screen and murder lurks round every corner; the heroes as powerless to intervene as they are to resist investigating...

Born in Rome, Argento was the son of a film producer, Salvatore Argento, and a Brazilian-born photographer, Elda Luxardo. Beginning his career as a newspaper columnist/critic, he first turned to screenwriting, collaborating with Bernardo Bertolucci on Sergio Leone's classic spaghetti Western *Once Upon a Time in the West* (1969). His directorial debut, *The Bird with the Crystal Plumage* (1970), was a highly stylized *giallo* – a peculiarly Italian genre that is part sophisticated whodunnit, part overheated slasher. More *gialli* followed, culminating in *Deep Red* (1975), which sees pianist David Hemmings trailing a half-seen killer through a rotten, haunted Rome.

*Suspiria* (1977), *Inferno* (1980) and *Phenomena* (1985) mixed *giallo* plots with spiralling supernatural elements. Set in a German dance academy run by a coven of witches, *Suspiria* was shot in gaudy primary colours (using the same Technicolor printing process as *The Wizard of Oz*, 1939) and soundtracked with gale-force fury by prog-rockers Goblin. As ever, Argento delights in sadistic set pieces that favour sensation over sense. Maggots rain from the ceiling, secret passages lead to hidden

## FILMS TO SEE

★ *The Bird with the Crystal Plumage* (1970)
★ *Deep Red* (1975)
★ *Suspiria* (1977)
★ *Tenebrae* (1982)
★ *Opera* (1987)

## DID YOU KNOW?

In films such as *Deep Red* and *Tenebrae* it is Argento's hands we see wearing the murderer's gloves. 'I love all my killers,' he has explained.

lairs, and one poor student stumbles into a room full of barbed wire. In Argento's world, as in dreams, the fabric of the buildings themselves can't be trusted.

Even more conventional efforts such as *Tenebrae* (1982) and *Opera* (1987) have a feverish quality that pulls viewers in, like the characters themselves. Often artists and always underprepared for the evils they discover, Argento's heroes find themselves sucked into the vortex, as if it is the artistic mind itself that leads them into darkness. He should know. 'Sometimes I think the director of any picture is insane, at least while he's making it,' he explains in Maitland McDonagh's aptly named *Broken Mirrors/Broken Minds*. On the basis of works as hallucinatory as *Suspiria* and *Deep Red*, there is no cure.

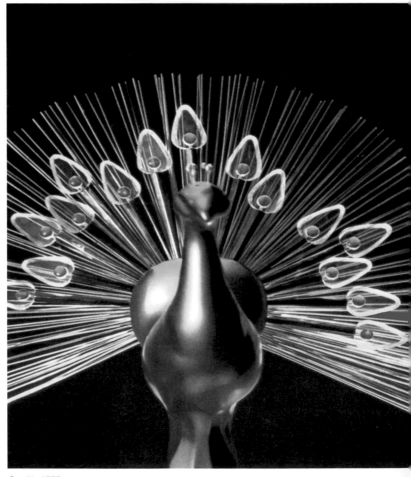

*Suspiria*, 1977

> Bad luck isn't brought
> by broken mirrors, but by
> broken minds.

 *SUSPIRIA*

Since the 1990s Argento's films have been increasingly poorly received by critics, proving hallucinatory for all the wrong reasons. Even his fans must have pinched themselves during the loopy *Mother of Tears* (2007), a too-little-too-late sequel to *Suspiria* and *Inferno*, and the beyond parody *Giallo* (2009). Ironically, his later misfires have only made his earlier work burn brighter. ★

# DARREN
# **A**RONOFSKY

AMERICAN
BORN 1969

Darren Aronofsky makes the films that no one else wants to. Whether sci-fi, drama or horror, or a curdled combination of all three, they tackle difficult, unfashionable subjects such as maths and ballet, and feature obsessives seeking enlightenment – or oblivion – while refusing to process the hardships of real life. The results should be frustrating, but actually they are beautiful.

Born in Brooklyn, New York, to a conservative Jewish family, Aronofsky studied film and social anthropology at Harvard, then directing at the American Film Institute. The latter paid off handsomely – his feature debut, Lynchian head-trip *Pi* (1998), which he also co-wrote, won a best director award at the Sundance Film Festival, despite being made for just $60,000. Shot in gorgeously granulated black and white, it centres on an increasingly unhinged mathematician's search for the meaning of life through numbers. It was hardly box-office dynamite, but Aronofsky's hyper-stylized direction made it unmissable.

The same goes for *Requiem for a Dream* (2000), a harrowing study of heroin addiction based on Hubert Selby, Jr's 1978 novel. It may well be Aronofsky's masterpiece, if you can bear to sit through the parade of shattered dreams and ruined bodies. He followed it with *The Fountain* (2006), a centuries-spanning rumination on mortality that felt hand-made rather than Hollywood-forged. The troubled production and

## FILMS TO SEE

★ *Pi* (1998)
★ *Requiem for a Dream* (2000)
★ *The Fountain* (2006)
★ *The Wrestler* (2008)
★ *Black Swan* (2010)

## DID YOU KNOW?

No stranger to controversy, Aronofksy fell foul of the Motion Picture Association of America ratings board over *Requiem*'s distressing sex scenes; Natalie Portman's dance double on *Black Swan* over a perceived lack of credit; and the entire Christian Right over *Noah*.

I'm trying to understand our world. I don't deal with petty materialists like you.

 *Pi*

mixed reception might have deterred lesser talents, but Aronofsky came back fighting with two wildly different yet thematically twinned works. A low-key drama starring Hollywood *persona non grata* Mickey Rourke as a battle-worn fighter who can't throw in the towel, *The Wrestler* (2008) was an object lesson in crippling pathos. *Black Swan* (2010) followed another lost soul to the brink, this time Natalie Portman's brittle ballerina, who finds herself haunted by her evil doppelgänger. The result was the most critically garlanded horror film since *The Exorcist* (1973).

*Requiem for a Dream, 2000*

Never exactly a careerist, Aronofsky's next work was another tough sell: a big-budget CG-heavy retelling of the biblical story of *Noah* (2014). If religious groups were unhappy, God didn't seem best pleased either – the shoot was disrupted by 2012's Hurricane Sandy. Although it feels like a leftfield choice, Noah himself fits rather well into Aronofsky's cast of dedicated loners, who try to place order on the chaos of the world and, gloriously, fail. Long may they continue. ★

*Black Swan, 2010*

# INGMAR
# **B**ERGMAN

SWEDISH

1918–2007

The ultimate director's director, Ingmar Bergman was, quietly, one of the most original and influential film-makers of all time. Indeed, many of the greats cite him as a personal favourite, and his face appears on Sweden's 200-kronor banknotes.

Born in Uppsala, Sweden, to a Lutheran minister and a nurse – which probably accounts for his obsession with mortality and punishment – the young Bergman swapped his toy soldiers for a magic lantern (a rudimentary projector) and performed Strindberg plays with shadows and puppets. He retained a love of theatre throughout his life, putting on some 200 plays, and moving into film with Alf Sjöberg's *Torment* (1944), on which he was writer and assistant director. International recognition arrived with his own *Smiles of a Summer Night* (1955), a comedy, though he would come to be known for deathly serious works such as *The Seventh Seal* (1957), *Wild Strawberries* (1957), *Persona* (1966) and *Fanny and Alexander* (1982). Often, he used a stock company of actors including Max von Sydow, and shot on the otherworldly island of Fårö.

Even if you haven't seen his films, you have felt their icy fingers across the pop-cultural spectrum. *The Seventh Seal*'s chess match between Death and a medieval knight (von Sydow) has been parodied by everyone from Monty Python to the Muppets; *Smiles* informed both Stephen Sondheim's musical *A Little Night Music*

## FILMS TO SEE

★ *The Seventh Seal* (1957)
★ *Wild Strawberries* (1957)
★ *The Virgin Spring* (1960)
★ *Persona* (1966)
★ *Fanny and Alexander* (1982)

## DID YOU KNOW?

Stanley Kubrick was so moved by *Wild Strawberries* that he wrote to Bergman proclaiming: 'Your vision of life has moved me deeply, much more deeply than I have ever been moved by any films. I believe you are the greatest film-maker at work today.'

Le nouveau film de
**INGMAR BERGMAN**

# PERSONA

**BIBI ANDERSSON**
**LIV ULLMANN**

Distribué par **LES ARTISTES ASSOCIES**

*Wild Strawberries,* 1957

No form of art goes beyond ordinary consciousness as film does, straight to our emotions.

 INGMAR BERGMAN

(1973) and Woody Allen's *A Midsummer Night's Sex Comedy* (1982); and *The Virgin Spring* (1960), a sombre tale of rape and vengeance, inspired Wes Craven's video nasty *The Last House on the Left* (1972). The extraordinary near-silent dream sequence that crowns *Wild Strawberries*, which follows an old man (company regular Victor Sjöström) along a deserted, eerily sunlit street as a carriage spills a coffin at his feet, summed up Bergman's preoccupations – death, stasis, the absence of god – and echoes in the surreal works of David Lynch and others.

For all his metaphysical disquiet, Bergman died peacefully, in his sleep, on Fårö, at the ripe old age of 89. ★

*Persona,* 1936

# KATHRYN **B**IGELOW

AMERICAN
BORN 1951

In the gender-restrictive world of action cinema, Kathryn Bigelow has taken on the Hollywood patriarchy and succeeded, her films not only delivering macho spectacle, but deconstructing it, too. Born in San Carlos, California, she studied fine art, then film under cultural theorist Susan Sontag, before delivering her first salvo, *The Set-Up* (1978), a short showing two men fighting while intellectuals pick apart what we are seeing in voiceover. Her best work continues this line of enquiry, centring on fringe groups engaged in conflicts without end.

In her feature debut, *The Loveless (*1982), co-directed with Monty Montgomery, it is Willem Dafoe's bikers; in *Near Dark* (1987) it is Lance Henriksen's nomadic vampires. *Blue Steel* (1989) showed rookie cop Jamie Lee Curtis fighting to survive in a man's world, and tempts an autobiographical reading, but it was the one-two punch of *Point Break* (1991) and *Strange Days* (1995) that crystallized Bigelow's themes. In the former, a gloriously over-pumped testosterone fest, undercover cop Keanu Reeves becomes enamoured with Patrick Swayze's bank-robbing surfers. In the latter, an ambitious sci-fi, Ralph Fiennes sells second-hand memory recordings that users can experience vicariously, like action junkies seeking the next high. The opening Steadicam sequence, which shows a botched robbery entirely from the robber's point of view, is a master class in immersive film-making.

## FILMS TO SEE

★ *Near Dark* (1987)
★ *Point Break* (1991)
★ *Strange Days* (1995)
★ *The Hurt Locker* (2008)
★ *Zero Dark Thirty* (2012)

## DID YOU KNOW?

Both *The Hurt Locker* and *Zero Dark Thirty* were based on extensive research by journalist Mark Boal. The US government sued the CIA for allegedly allowing Bigelow and Boal access to classified information regarding the Bin Laden operation.

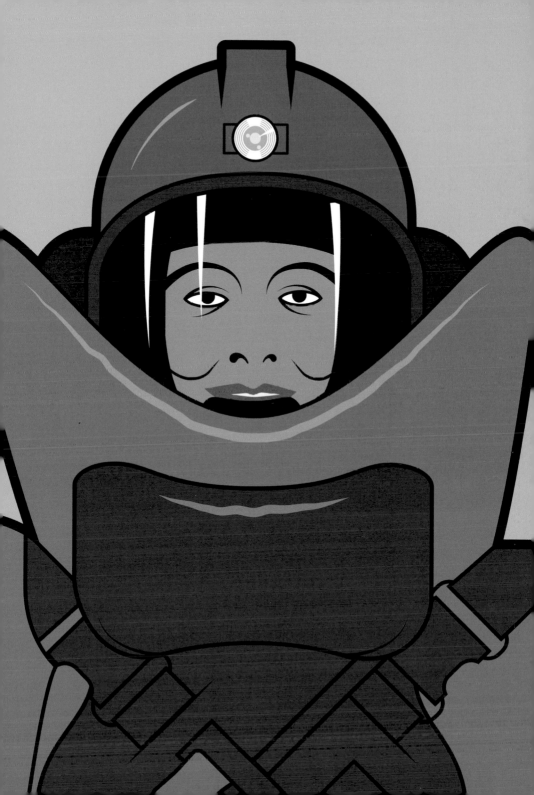

> War's dirty little secret is that
> some men love it.

KATHRYN BIGELOW

In *The Hurt Locker* (2008) it is war itself that is the addictive drug, dragging bomb-disposal expert Jeremy Renner back to the Iraqi frontline for another fix no matter what the cost. *The Hurt Locker*'s companion piece, *Zero Dark Thirty* (2012), is about the CIA's relentless hunt for Osama Bin Laden, torture and all, and was equally wired into but also wary of the evil that men do in such situations. At the 82nd Academy Awards, Bigelow beat ex-husband and Tinseltown alpha male James Cameron to the Best Director Oscar with *The Hurt Locker*, becoming the first woman ever to win. ★

*Zero Dark Thirty*, 2012

*Strange Days*, 1995

# DANNY
# **B**OYLE

BRITISH
BORN 1956

There is something irrepressible about Danny Boyle's work: a 'Lust for Life', to quote *Trainspotting*'s (1996) surging soundtrack featuring Iggy Pop's 1977 song. Flitting from genre to genre, each of his films is alive with possibility. From *Trainspotting*'s opening sprint from the law, to the Bollywood dance number closing *Slumdog Millionaire* (2008), these are movies that really move. Even *127 Hours* (2010), the true-life tale of a man with his arm stuck under a rock, has an over-caffeinated energy all its own.

Brought up in a working-class Irish Catholic household in Radcliffe, Lancashire, Boyle saw Francis Ford Coppola's *Apocalypse Now* (1979) and found himself 'sandblasted by the power of cinema', as he told journalist Robert K Elder. He directed theatre for the Royal Shakespeare Company, among others, and produced Alan Clarke's short *Elephant* (1989), before embarking on his own TV and films. *Shallow Grave* (1994) is a vicious little tale of flatmates fighting over a windfall, but it showcased Boyle's largesse, especially when they start spending. *Trainspotting* turned Irvine Welsh's novel of Edinburgh heroin addicts into an amphetamized Britpop masterpiece.

Whether lovers on the run in *A Life Less Ordinary* (1997), restless travellers in *The Beach* (2000) or sprinting 'zombies' in *28 Days Later* (2002), Boyle's characters refuse to sit still – even the gentle *Millions* (2004) becomes a race against time for two schoolboys who stumble across a fortune. No wonder Boyle disliked making the

## FILMS TO SEE
★ *Shallow Grave* (1994)
★ *Trainspotting* (1996)
★ *Sunshine* (2007)
★ *Slumdog Millionaire* (2008)
★ *127 Hours* (2010)

## DID YOU KNOW?
Like fellow directors Martin Scorsese, John Woo and M Night Shyamalan, Boyle intended to join the priesthood before he discovered films. 'It's basically the same job,' he explained to *The Times*, 'poncing around, telling people what to think.'

gorgeous *Sunshine* (2007), a tribute to the life-giving qualities of light: the locked-down sci-fi setting proved too restrictive for his roving camera.

With *Slumdog Millionaire*, the rags-to-riches tale of a Mumbai orphan playing a high-stakes TV quiz show, Boyle hit the Oscar jackpot: the film was nominated for ten Academy Awards and won eight, including Best Director. Criticized by some for what was seen as its heavily Westernized view of India, it nonetheless enjoyed massive

worldwide success, grossing $2.2 million on its opening weekend in China alone. Boyle kept up the momentum with *127 Hours*, nominated for six Academy Awards, and then headed back to Blighty to make *Trance* (2013), a psycho-thriller that travels at several times the speed of sense. Perhaps he works best when he is at the centre of the maelstrom, like the character in *Sunshine* who relaxes amid crashing, computer-generated seas, reasoning, 'The waves make me feel peaceful.' ★

*Trainspotting, 1996*

We called him Mother Superior on account of the length of his habit.

 *TRAINSPOTTING*

# TIM
# BURTON

AMERICAN
BORN 1958

'There's nothing wrong with Victor,' says young Master Frankenstein's mum in Tim Burton's animated feature *Frankenweenie* (2012). 'He's just in his own world.' You can imagine Mrs Burton saying the same of her son, an introverted teen who shot his own stop-motion experiments in their Burbank, California, backyard.

Taking an animator's apprenticeship at ultra-conservative Disney, Burton worked on releases such as *The Black Cauldron* (1985), which Disney disowned for being too dark. After gothic shorts such as *Vincent* (1982), featuring the dulcet tones of horror legend Vincent Price, and the original *Frankenweenie* (1984), Disney disowned Burton, too, who made his feature debut, *Pee-Wee's Big Adventure* (1985), for cult children's entertainer Pee-Wee Herman instead.

Retaining an animator's eye for detail, Burton began creating dazzlingly designed, but internally consistent, otherworlds such as the anarchic afterlife depicted in horror-comedy *Beetlejuice* (1988). *Batman* (1989) took Burton's brooding visuals into blockbuster territory, while Grimm romance *Edward Scissorhands* (1990), starring Johnny Depp as a Frankenstein's Monster-style outcast, was a beguiling snow globe of a film – all pastel-perfect suburbs crowned by a Hammer-horror castle.

Since then, Burton has dabbled with stop-motion animation, on Disney's *The Nightmare before Christmas* (1993); with the subject of gothic classics such

## FILMS TO SEE
★ *Beetlejuice* (1988)
★ *Batman* (1989)
★ *Edward Scissorhands* (1990)
★ *Ed Wood* (1994)
★ *Sweeney Todd: The Demon Barber of Fleet Street* (2007)

## DID YOU KNOW?
Burton keeps his friends close. Johnny Depp, the godfather of his son, has starred in eight of his films; Helena Bonham Carter, his ex-partner, has appeared in seven; while Hammer star Christopher Lee, his idol, can be seen – or heard – in six.

These aren't my rules.
Come to think of it,
I don't have any rules.

  *BEETLEJUICE*

as *Sleepy Hollow* (1999) and *Sweeney Todd: The Demon Barber of Fleet Street* (2007); and with creepy children's fiction, mounting Day-Glo adaptations of Roald Dahl's *Charlie and the Chocolate Factory* (2005) as well as the Lewis Carroll classic, *Alice in Wonderland* (2010).

Though most of his work is emphatically not for children, it has a youthful sense of wonder, as if he still has one hand in his Halloween candy stash. Most of all, he identifies with dreamers such as the eponymous, epically failed film director in *Ed Wood* (1994) and the myth-making patriarch of *Big Fish* (2003); men who make up their own alluring universes and, dissatisfied with reality, decide to stay there. ★

*Batman,* 1989

*Edward Scissorhands,* 1990

# JANE
# **C**AMPION

NEW ZEALAND
BORN 1954

Jane Campion's credentials speak for themselves: the New Zealand-born director was the first (and so far only) woman to win the Cannes Film Festival's top prize, the Palme d'Or, and the second to be nominated for the Best Director Oscar, both for *The Piano* (1993). Her films do, too, albeit softly. Calm on the surface, they feature powerful undertows of emotion.

Born into a family of theatre lovers, Campion studied anthropology in her home town, Wellington, then painting and, later, film in Sydney, Australia, where she now resides. One of her first shorts, *Peel: An Exercise in Discipline* (1982), won its category's Palme d'Or as well, making her the first woman to win that, too, and its follow-up, *A Girl's Own Story* (1984), provides a good summary of her subtly feminist oeuvre. Her first feature, *Sweetie* (1989), and TV miniseries *An Angel at My Table* (1990), about Kiwi poet Janet Frame, were seen through the eyes of damaged young women empowered by art. The same goes for *The Piano*, which set Campion on the world stage and won her a Best Screenwriting Oscar.

A sensuous work about Ada (Holly Hunter), a mute 19th-century mother sold in marriage to a New Zealand frontiersman (Sam Neill), it follows Ada's efforts to reclaim her piano – her voice – which has been left abandoned on a barren shore. The idea of women rendered powerless by hypocrisies of their times reoccurred in Henry James

## FILMS TO SEE
★ *Sweetie* (1989)
★ *The Piano* (1993)
★ *The Portrait of a Lady* (1996)
★ *Holy Smoke!* (1999)
★ *Bright Star* (2009)

## DID YOU KNOW?
The career-changing role of Ada in *The Piano* proved surprisingly difficult to cast. Sigourney Weaver, Jennifer Jason Leigh and Isabelle Huppert all passed, before Hunter's dogged pursuit paid off.

42

adaptation *The Portrait of a Lady* (1996) and Keats biopic *Bright Star* (2009), which centres on Fanny Brawne, a woman who loved the poet but was forbidden to marry him because of his poor financial prospects. The battle of the sexes, in different forms, animates *Holy Smoke!* (1999), about a woman's spiritual awakening in India, and erotic thriller *In the Cut* (2003). Frustrated by the conservatism of the film industry, Campion's latest work, mystery *Top of the Lake* (2013), took her back to TV – and the wilds of New Zealand. As she told *The Telegraph*: 'Television is the new frontier.' ★

*Sweetie*, 1989

To deny women directors, as I suspect is happening in the States, is to deny the feminine vision.

 JANE CAMPION

*The Piano* 1993

# JOHN CARPENTER

AMERICAN
BORN 1948

With his rebellious streak, blue-collar leanings and fondness for disreputable genres, John Carpenter might scorn his inclusion in the canon of great directors. 'I'm like a good whore,' he's said, quoting hero John Wayne, 'I go where I'm pushed.' But that is disingenuous. Carpenter's muscular B-movies have an ingenuity and economy that inspired a generation the way John Ford, Howard Hawks and Alfred Hitchcock inspired him.

Born in Carthage, New York, Carpenter grew up in Kentucky, where the local boys beat him up for being different – inspiration, perhaps, for the siege movies he would become famous for. He moved to California to study cinema, winning praise for short films such as *Captain Voyeur* (1969), which would inform his later *Halloween* (1978), and Western-inflected *The Resurrection of Broncho Billy* (1970). His feature debut was the charmingly ramshackle sci-fi *Dark Star* (1974), which he wrote, directed, scored and edited, the latter under the pseudonym 'John T Chance', Wayne's character in Hawks's *Rio Bravo* (1959). The same film inspired urban warfare thriller *Assault on Precinct 13* (1976), the first of many tough-talking, take-no-prisoners flicks such as *Escape from New York* (1981) and *They Live* (1988).

Two in particular are matchless in their minimal perfection. *Halloween* all but invented the slasher film, its voyeuristic Panaglide point-of-view shots and silent, masked

## FILMS TO SEE

★ *Dark Star* (1974)
★ *Assault on Precinct 13* (1976)
★ *Halloween* (1978)
★ *Escape from New York* (1981)
★ *The Thing* (1982)

## DID YOU KNOW?

For *Big Trouble in Little China* (1986) Carpenter formed rock band the Coupe de Villes with *Halloween III: Season of the Witch* (1982) director Tommy Lee Wallace and Nick Castle, who played Michael Myers.

CARPENTER

*Halloween,* 1978

Look at that, two cops wishing
me luck. I'm doomed.

 *ASSAULT ON PRECINCT 13*

killer (named Michael Myers after the film's UK distributor) becoming horror mainstays. The presence of Jamie Lee Curtis, daughter of Janet Leigh from *Psycho* (1960), is not the only nod to Hitchcock – the film is a master class in suspense.

Blood and guts were much more to the fore in gruesome sci-fi *The Thing* (1982). Based on the same source material as the Hawks-produced *The Thing from Another World* (1951), it concerns a shape-changing alien attacking Kurt Russell's Antarctic researchers. Rob Bottin's disgusting special effects are the stuff of nightmares, but it is the sense of poisonous paranoia that above all gives the film its power.

Carpenter may see himself as a workman-for-hire, but you can't set out to create cult classics like these, and you can't fake them. Indeed, the frequency with which his films have been remade – badly – underlines what a force to be reckoned with he is. ★

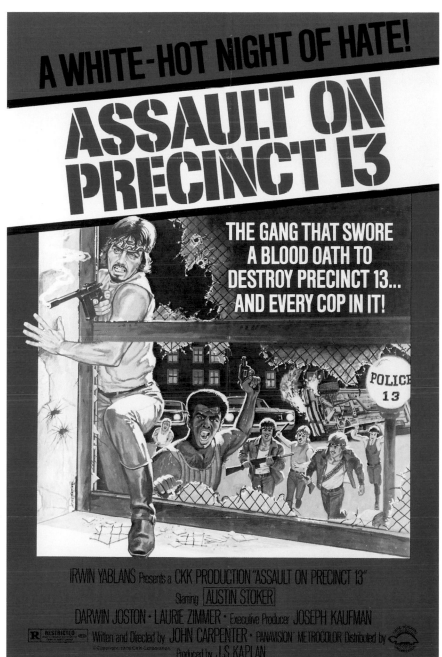

# CHARLIE
# **C**HAPLIN

BRITISH
1889–1977

Cinema's greatest clown more than fulfils the stereotype – there were tears as well as laughter; real pathos behind the pratfalls. A driven writer and director who became the highest-paid star in the world, Chaplin came from grinding poverty, spending time in London's workhouses and seeing his mother committed to a mental asylum as a teen. Perhaps this accounts for the self-sufficiency he sought.

After a childhood spent performing in music halls, Chaplin's big break came when touring America as part of Fred Karno's company (Stan Laurel was his understudy). The 19-year-old was spotted by Keystone Studios' scouts and made his first appearance on screen in *Making a Living* (1914). He began directing his own short films and developed his now legendary 'Tramp' persona: a silent, sad-eyed figure who always keeps trying, though buffeted by bad luck or, simply, gravity.

With actors Douglas Fairbanks and Mary Pickford and director D W Griffiths, Chaplin set up his own distribution company, United Artists, enjoying complete autonomy on features such as *The Kid* (1921), *City Lights* (1931), *Modern Times* (1936) and *The Great Dictator* (1940). But his controversial love life and alleged communist leanings saw him hounded out of the United States. He moved to Switzerland, ditched the Tramp, and diversified with more sophisticated comedies such as *Monsieur Verdoux* (1947) and *A Countess from Hong Kong* (1967).

## FILMS TO SEE
★ *The Kid* (1921)
★ *The Gold Rush* (1925)
★ *City Lights* (1931)
★ *Modern Times* (1936)
★ *The Great Dictator* (1940)

## DID YOU KNOW?
Months after he died, Chaplin's body was held to ransom by two thieves. A film about the incident, *The Price of Fame*, was released in 2014 with the Chaplin family's blessing. Charlie is now buried under reinforced concrete.

Failure is unimportant.
It takes courage to make
a fool of yourself.

 CHARLIE CHAPLIN

But sadness remained: a suicide attempt in *City Lights*; starvation in *The Gold Rush* (1925); and hardship all round. There was also a satiric bite. What made the misery funny was Chaplin's joy in the small things, such as the scene where his barber shaves a customer to classical music, as if conducting. *City Lights* has him parading in front of a manhole, almost falling in, but somehow staying up – a good metaphor for his entire career. ★

*The Gold Rush*, 1925

# JOEL & ETHAN
# COEN

AMERICAN
BORN 1954
& 1957

Roderick Jaynes, the Coen brothers' loyal editor, was nominated for Oscars for both *Fargo* (1996) and *No Country for Old Men* (2007). The kicker? He doesn't exist. Ignore the credits: Joel and Ethan write, direct, produce and edit their own films. Jaynes is just another example of how these arch contrarians have sneaked into the Hollywood hierarchy without compromising their quirks – or their mystique.

Ever since childhood, when Joel raised money to buy a camera by mowing the lawns of suburban Minneapolis, the Coens have trod a seemingly random trail to the top. Their debut, *Blood Simple* (1984), was a gritty noir. Next came wacky comedy *Raising Arizona* (1987). *Miller's Crossing* (1990) was a gangster film, *Barton Fink* (1991), a Hollywood head-scratcher, *The Big Lebowski* (1998), a little of both. Unlikely remakes such as *True Grit* (2010) butted heads with *O Brother, Where Art Thou?* (2000), a Depression-era bluegrass musical based on Homer's *The Odyssey*. There is no telling what they are going to do next.

The Coens' characters must feel the same way. Whether luckless anti-heroes or loveable losers, they find themselves on wild-goose chases, ending back where they began, like Oscar Isaac's folk singer in *Inside Llewyn Davies* (2013). Try as they might, they can't escape destiny – as unforgettably embodied by Javier Bardem's hideously

## FILMS TO SEE
★ *Miller's Crossing* (1990)
★ *Fargo* (1996)
★ *The Big Lebowski* (1998)
★ *No Country for Old Men* (2007)
★ *Inside Llewyn Davis* (2013)

## DID YOU KNOW?
When writing, the Coens start with a scene instead of an outline. If they can think of the next scene, they write the script until it is finished. If not, they start another script – hence *Barton Fink* was started and finished during the writing of *Miller's Crossing*.

*Fargo*, 1996

If the rule you followed brought you to this, of what use was the rule?

 *NO COUNTRY FOR OLD MEN*

coiffed, coin-tossing assassin in *No Country for Old Men*. Theirs are chaotic, amoral worlds, where bad things happen to good people, and vice versa.

To keep us guessing, the brothers are happy to leave plot threads dangling. *The Big Lebowski* makes mention of a huge bowling contest that never happens; major characters in *No Country for Old Men* meet their (presumably messy) fates off screen; and who knows what becomes of the ransom money so bitterly fought for in *Fargo*? One of the most infamous Coen tricks was to introduce the events of *Fargo* as 'based on a true story' when they are not in the least. But it is just another way of saying, 'We're not going to give you what you expect, but something better.' Jaynes, you imagine, would approve. ★

*The Big Lebowski, 1998*

# FRANCIS FORD
# **C**OPPOLA

AMERICAN
BORN 1939

Francis Ford Coppola is not a man to do things by halves. An ebullient Italian American who favours the largest of canvases, he became the don of 1970s New Hollywood cinema, making grandiose films that explored alternative power structures: the Mafia in *The Godfather Trilogy* (1972–90), a military dictatorship in *Apocalypse Now* (1979). He even tried to create one himself, establishing his own studio, Zoetrope. But few of his 1970s contemporaries flew higher or crashed harder.

Suffering from polio as a child in Detroit, the young Coppola stayed home and made 8mm movies because he wasn't allowed outside. After studying film in California, he worked for B-movie supremo Roger Corman, writing/directing horror film *Dementia 13* (1963) in a matter of days. Studio jobs such as *You're a Big Boy Now* (1966) followed, but it was his Oscar-winning script for *Patton* (1970) that really opened doors.

Based on Mario Puzo's pulp novel about a Sicilian crime syndicate, *The Godfather* (1972) elevated the material until it felt positively operatic, with iconic performances from Marlon Brando and Al Pacino, Gordon Willis's inky deep-focus photography and Nino Rota's mournful score combining to create a masterpiece. Somehow, he repeated the magic with *The Godfather Part II* (1974). That year he received two nominations for the Best Picture Oscar – which, needless to say, he won. The other film, conspiracy thriller *The Conversation* (1974), took home the Palme d'Or instead.

## FILMS TO SEE

★ *The Godfather* (1972)
★ *The Godfather Part II* (1974)
★ *The Conversation* (1974)
★ *Apocalypse Now* (1979)
★ *Rumble Fish* (1983)

## DID YOU KNOW?

Coppola has a cameo in *Apocalypse Now*, as the bossy war reporter telling troops, 'Don't look at the camera!' Sister Talia Shire has a major role in *The Godfather Trilogy*, while daughter Sofia's performance in *The Godfather Part III* was considered the film's undoing.

My father made him an offer
he couldn't refuse.

  *THE GODFATHER*

Having pondered the modern demagogue for so long, Coppola almost became one himself. *Apocalypse Now* (1979), based on Joseph Conrad's novel *Heart of Darkness*, saw the director effectively restaging the Vietnam War in the Philippines, and nearly killing himself in the process. 'We were in the jungle, there were too many of us, we had access to too much money, too much equipment and little by little, we went insane,' he told documentary makers, which could be a line from the film.

Did he ever really recover? Zoetrope went bankrupt, accomplished dramas such as *Rumble Fish* (1983) were overshadowed by flops such as *The Cotton Club* (1984), *The Godfather Part III* (1990) floundered, and Coppola became, effectively, a studio gun-for-hire, which can't have been part of the plan. Elsewhere his appetite for excess flourishes: the Coppola brand has grown to include vineyards, pasta sauce and holiday resorts. ★

*Rumble Fish*, 1983

*The Godfather*, 1972

# DAVID
# CRONENBERG

CANADIAN
BORN 1943

For a writer-director with such a breathtaking singularity of vision, the notion of fusion crops up over and over again in Cronenberg's work. It is almost as if he were able to step into one of the telepods in *The Fly* (1986) with a new concept or contributor, then emerge combined, a completely new being. Born in Toronto to progressive middle-class parents, Cronenberg studied science at university, before switching to English literature, discovering film, and graduating top of the class. The tension between these subjects would form the backbone of a career encompassing everything from B-movies to literary adaptations, each made unmistakeably his own.

From venereal horror *Shivers* (1975) to eye-popping sci-fi *Scanners* (1981), Cronenberg's first commercial forays fused cerebral chills with sudden spurts of gore, his ideas made flesh in icky, glistening special effects. *Videodrome* (1983), his most sophisticated work of the period, posits a world where images of sexual violence can cause physical growths. A key sequence has seedy TV executive James Woods, addicted to pornography, growing a vaginal video slot in his stomach to receive still more hard-core material. 'Long live the new flesh!' is the film's mantra, but it could be Cronenberg's.

A move to Hollywood prompted his next 'fusions' – with A-list stars. Though not traditionally considered an actors' director, Cronenberg coaxed eccentric,

## FILMS TO SEE
★ *Videodrome* (1983)
★ *The Dead Zone* (1983)
★ *The Fly* (1986)
★ *Dead Ringers* (1988)
★ *A History of Violence* (2005)

## DID YOU KNOW?
Cronenberg appears as a silent hit man in *To Die For* (1995), a gentle boss in *Last Night* (1998), and an evil scientist in *Jason X* (2002). *The Fly* provided his most pertinent cameo: a gynaecologist in a grue-filled nightmare.

> Television is reality, and reality is less than television.

 *VIDEODROME*

career-best performances from Christopher Walken (in *The Dead Zone*, 1983), Jeff Goldblum (in *The Fly*) and Jeremy Irons (in *Dead Ringers*, 1988) as men whose 'gifts' lead them to ruin. Walken played a coma survivor cursed with second sight; Goldblum an inventor genetically spliced with an insect; Irons a pair of twins with one soul split between them. Each film resonates with the tragedy of lives unlived.

Turning his attentions back to literature, Cronenberg fused his sensibilities with authors such as William S Burroughs on the supposedly unfilmable *Naked Lunch* (1991), J G Ballard on the censor-baiting *Crash* (1996) and Patrick McGrath on the schizophrenia-themed *Spider* (2002). Even a later shift towards the mainstream did not dilute his themes. *A History of Violence* (2005) and *Eastern Promises* (2007) may be gangster films, but they are also Cronenberg films; Hollywood satire *Maps to the Stars* (2014) examines Tinseltown grotesques under the same unforgiving microscope; and his first novel, *Consumed* (2014), which equates technological fetishism with cannibalism, takes the Cronenberg canon full circle. ★

*The Fly*, 1986

# D TO F

DONEN
EISENSTEIN
FELLINI
FINCHER
FORD

# STANLEY
# DONEN

AMERICAN
BORN 1924

Was there ever a director who brought more joy to the screen? A Broadway dancer turned Hollywood choreographer, Donen made some of the best, and best-loved, musicals of all time.

Born in South Carolina and bullied in his youth, Donen retreated into movies, particularly musicals. Befriending Gene Kelly on a Broadway chorus line, he made his way to Hollywood, where the two co-directed *On the Town* (1949) featuring Kelly and Frank Sinatra as singing sailors let loose in New York. Despite their fractious relationship offscreen, onscreen Donen and Kelly's choreography was an effortless extension of the story. Think of Kelly's rapturous puddle-splashing in *Singin'*, billed as a 'Singin' Swingin' Glorious Feeling Technicolor Musical', or the roller-skating tap dance in *It's Always Fair Weather* (1955), 'a new musical to lift you right up to the blue skies'.

In order to bring the genre out of the theatre and into the cinema, Donen utilized real locations, jarring jump cuts and 360-degree pans, bringing in novel elements so that each dance number seemed made up on the spot. *Royal Wedding* (1951) used a revolving set to allow Astaire to dance across the 'ceiling' (a scene homaged in *Inception*, 2010). *Funny Face* divides the screen in three so Astaire, Audrey Hepburn and Kay Thompson can sing together while cavorting separately across Paris. Romantic comedy *Indiscreet* (1958), meanwhile, deployed a split-screen device

## FILMS TO SEE

★ *On the Town* (1949)
★ *Singin' in the Rain* (1952)
★ *It's Always Fair Weather* (1955)
★ *Funny Face* (1957)
★ *Charade* (1963)

## DID YOU KNOW?

Both Donen and Kelly married the same woman. Dancer Jeanne Coyne became the first Mrs Donen (of five), then the second Mrs Kelly (of three) nine years later. 'It was all pretty incestuous,' said Kelly, with some understatement.

*On the Town*, 1949

She can't act, she can't sing, she can't dance. A triple threat.

*SINGIN' IN THE RAIN*

to suggest unmarried lovers Cary Grant and Ingrid Bergman are in bed together (disallowed under the Hays Code), when in fact they are in different cities.

But there was bitter-sweetness as well. *Singin'* satirizes Hollywood pomposity, *Funny Face* mocks women's magazines, while *Fair Weather* is positively sour in places, particularly reunion song 'I Shouldn't Have Come'. As the public's taste for musicals soured, too, Donen diversified into thrillers, making *Charade* (1963), 'the best Hitchcock movie that Hitchcock never made', and sci-fi, with *Saturn 3* (1980). But it is his magical musicals to which fans (including Chaplin and Kubrick) return, looking for another shot of liquid sunshine. ★

*Singin' in the Rain*, 1952

# SERGEI
# **E**ISENSTEIN

RUSSIAN
1898–1948

Film director, writer and theorist Sergei Eisenstein pioneered the use of montage, an editing style by which images are cut together to imply a relationship between them. The experiments of his contemporary Lev Kuleshov illustrate the point. When a shot of a man's face was followed by a shot of a bowl of soup, audiences inferred that he was hungry. Eisenstein used the technique for political ends, drawing attention to what was happening in revolutionary Russia and the turbulent years that followed.

Eisenstein was born to a middle-class family in Riga, Latvia, but raised in St Petersburg, where he studied architecture and engineering – and it was the meticulous assembly of his films that mattered more than the stories they told. He made Red Army propaganda for the 1917 October Revolution, before moving into radical theatre and film. *Strike* (1925) was a true tale of a factory revolt. A famous montage intercuts shots of workers being gunned down by government troops with images of cattle being culled to devastating effect.

But his masterpiece was *Battleship Potemkin* (1925), about a naval rebellion in 1905, with its legendary Odessa Steps sequence homaged in Alfred Hitchcock's *Foreign Correspondent* (1940) and Brian De Palma's *The Untouchables* (1987), among others. In it, Czarist troops march unstoppably down the Odessa Steps, attacking women, children and – unforgettably – a baby in a pram. Stretched out in

## FILMS TO SEE

★ *Strike* (1925)
★ *Battleship Potemkin* (1925)
★ *October* (1928)
★ *Alexander Nevsky* (1938)
★ *Ivan the Terrible Parts I & II*
  (1944 & 1958)

## DID YOU KNOW?

While in Hollywood, Eisenstein befriended Charlie Chaplin – which can't have helped the latter refute those communist allegations. Chaplin's work, he thought, saw 'things most terrible, most pitiful, most tragic through the eyes of a laughing child'.

*Battleship Potemkin,* 1925

Language is much closer to
film than painting is.

 SERGEI EISENSTEIN

montage, the oppression seems endless, the violence indiscriminate. Goebbels thought the film 'marvellous' propaganda; no matter that the Steps massacre didn't actually happen.

Eisenstein made *October* (1928) for the Revolution's anniversary, then travelled to Europe, Hollywood and Mexico, leaving failed projects in his wake. Returning home to teach film theory, he made historical biopic *Alexander Nevsky* (1938), a thinly veiled attack on the Nazis, which Joseph Stalin banned after the Nazi–Soviet Pact of 1939. Eisenstein's *Ivan the Terrible Part I* (1944) won the Soviet leader's approval for its depiction of a national hero. But, ever the agitator, Eisenstein's *Part II* showed how quickly heroes turn into despots. Stalin was furious, and the film was not released until 1958, ten years after the film-maker died. *Part III* was not completed and has been mostly destroyed. ★

*Ivan the Terrible Part I,* 1944

# FEDERICO
# **F**ELLINI

ITALIAN
1920–93

Federico Fellini's black-and-white visions of *bella Italia* are so alluring he might have been employed by the tourist board. They also made Hollywood view foreign films in a different light, where previously it had barely viewed them at all.

Born in Rimini, to a baker and his bourgeois wife – a class clash that would animate his work – Fellini loved drawing. As a student in Rome he sold caricatures of restaurant patrons to scrape by, eventually finding work writing humorous articles and sketches for magazines, radio and, ultimately, films. His big break came when Roberto Rossellini, a neo-realist director (Italy's answer to Britain's kitchen-sink genre), co-opted him for the script of *Rome, Open City* (1945), and he made his directorial debut with *Variety Lights* (1950), a romantic drama set among vaudevillians. It was a bizarre apprenticeship, to say the least, but the mix of the theatrical and society gossip would infuse classics such as *La strada* (1954), about a circus strongman, and *La dolce vita* (1960), a tale of glamorous actors cutting loose in Rome.

Drawing from his own life, and dreams, Fellini often worked without a finished screenplay. *Il bidone* (1955) was based on anecdotes told to him by a thief; *Nights of Cabiria* (1957) on those of a local prostitute. The genesis of *8½* (1963), a surreal tale of a director adrift in his own movie, came to him when he lost sight of the film he intended to make. Its working title, *La bella confusione* ('The Beautiful Confusion'), proved

## FILMS TO SEE
★ *La strada* (1954)
★ *La dolce vita* (1960)
★ *8½* (1963)
★ *Fellini Satyricon* (1969)
★ *Amarcord* (1973)

## DID YOU KNOW?
The traffic-jam dream that begins *8½* inspired the hellish opening sequence of Joel Schumacher's *Falling Down* (1993) and the video for REM's 'Everybody Hurts' (1992).

*La dolce vita*, 1960

more than apt. It got its eventual title because for Fellini it was film number 8.5. He had made six features and two short film segments (which added up to one whole) and co-directed another (the half). Later works such as *Juliet of the Spirits* (1965), inspired by an LSD trip the director took, *Fellini Satyricon* (1969), and *Amarcord* (1973), about a year in the life of a Rimini village, continued this self-reflexive trend.

Even if I set out to make a film about a fillet of sole, it would be about me.

**99** FEDERICO FELLINI

Fellini won five Oscars over the course of his career, and his influence is still felt to this day in works as diverse as Maury Yeston's musical *Nine* (1982), which features a Fellini-esque director, and Peter Greenaway's film *8½ Women* (1999), among others. Indeed, Rimini's Federico Fellini International Airport was renamed in his honour, so passengers can set off on their very own flights of fancy. ★

*La strada*, 1954

# DAVID
# **F**INCHER

AMERICAN
BORN 1962

'This guy's methodical, exacting, and worst of all, patient,' says detective Morgan Freeman in *Se7en* (1995) of the serial killer he's tracking. 'He's a nut-bag!' counters partner Brad Pitt. Known for shooting take after take – up to 100 on *The Social Network* (2010); a positively relaxed 50 on *Gone Girl* (2014) – Fincher makes precise, oppressive films about the play between control and anarchy.

Growing up in Colorado, California and Oregon, Fincher worked his way up the movie ranks from production assistant at Korty Films to assistant cameraman at George Lucas's special-effects house, Industrial Light and Magic, where he worked on *Return of the Jedi* (1983). He left to direct commercials and music videos, making his feature debut with *Alien 3* (1992), a troubled film in which the chaos remained largely offscreen. 'To this day,' he told the *Guardian*, 'no one hates it more than me.'

Ink-black thrillers *Se7en* and *The Game* (1997) were followed by *Fight Club* (1999), a ferocious satire on millennial malaise, which saw Edward Norton's everyman falling under the spell of Pitt's idealized anarchist. Likewise, *Zodiac* (2007) recounts the real-life tale of how a *San Francisco Chronicle* cartoonist (Jake Gyllenhaal) ruined his life trying to solve riddles left by the eponymous murderer. Whether fight clubs or Facebook (as in *The Social Network*), the pattern of bored, limited men unleashing forces they can't contain continues through Fincher's oeuvre, the chaos

## FILMS TO SEE

★ *Se7en* (1995)
★ *The Game* (1997)
★ *Fight Club* (1999)
★ *Zodiac* (2007)
★ *The Social Network* (2010)

## DID YOU KNOW?

Though critically lauded, Fincher's works often do better with obsessive viewers than they do at the box office. *Fight Club* made a disappointing $37 million, but inspired fans to start their own bare-knuckle boxing groups.

It's only after we've lost everything that we're free to do anything.

 *FIGHT CLUB*

matched (or at least mapped) by his visual dynamism. Hitchcockian home-invasion thriller *Panic Room* (2003) features a shot that floats impossibly through the house as burglars break in; F Scott Fitzgerald short-story adaptation *The Curious Case of Benjamin Button* (2008) shows a battle running backwards.

Perhaps Fincher needs control because his characters don't have it, their panic rooms proving useless; their detective skills failing them. Ultimately, he seems to be saying, there is no point being methodical, exacting or patient, because the nut-bags always win. ★

*Fight Club,* 1999

*Gone Girl*, 2014

# JOHN **F**ORD

AMERICAN
1894–1973

With his trademark eye patch and pipe, John Ford casts an imposing figure over Hollywood history. A no-nonsense director of plain-speaking Westerns and dramas, Ford had much to say about the changing landscapes of America, even as he kept returning to the craggy constancy of Arizona's Monument Valley.

Born John Martin 'Jack' Feeney to Irish immigrants in Maine, Ford followed his older brother Francis to Hollywood. He changed his name and rose from stunt double to director, churning out dozens of silent pictures, most of them now lost. His first hit was *The Iron Horse* (1924), about the building of the First Transcontinental Railroad. How the West was won, and what was lost in the process, was a topic that would preoccupy him through 50 years and 140 films.

Set during the Irish War of Independence, *The Informer* (1935) won Ford the first of his six Oscars – none of which was for Westerns such as *Stagecoach* (1939), which revitalized the genre and made John Wayne a star. *The Grapes of Wrath* (1940) and *How Green Was My Valley* (1941) explored poverty in Depression-era California and a Welsh mining community respectively, while romantic drama *The Quiet Man* (1952) took Ford back to Ireland. But it was late-period oaters such as *The Searchers* (1956) and *The Man Who Shot Liberty Valance* (1962) that best summed up his themes: the dying of the old ways, the battle between civilization and savagery, and the tragedy

## FILMS TO SEE
★ *Stagecoach* (1939)
★ *The Grapes of Wrath* (1940)
★ *How Green Was My Valley* (1941)
★ *The Searchers* (1956)
★ *The Man Who Shot Liberty Valance* (1962)

## DID YOU KNOW?
Ford makes a brief appearance in D W Griffith's pioneering – but gallopingly racist – epic *The Birth of a Nation* (1915), as a Klansman. It inspired the Klan scene in Tarantino's *Django Unchained* (2012).

*The Searchers*, 1956

It is easier to get an actor to be a cowboy than to get a cowboy to be an actor.

JOHN FORD

of good men turned to violence. The latter was something he must have experienced first-hand during the Omaha Beach landings, where he lead a navy photographic unit.

In Ford's work, 'civilization' comes at a price (usually bloodshed), and the characters can't escape the wilderness – encapsulated in *The Searchers*' opening image of Wayne, seen from inside a silhouetted homestead, riding through Monument Valley's unforgiving sprawl. But there is hope, too. *Liberty* sees the frontier town of Shinbone transformed from a 'wilderness' to a 'garden', and the stoic last words of Ma Joad (Jane Darwell) in *Grapes*: 'They can't wipe us out; they can't lick us. We'll go on forever, Pa, 'cause we're the people,' are as much a promise as a prayer. ★

# G to K

GODARD

HERZOG

HITCHCOCK

IÑÁRRITU

JEUNET

KIEŚLOWSKI

KUBRICK

KUROSAWA

# JEAN-LUC GODARD

FRENCH-SWISS
BORN 1930

The French writer-directors of the 1950s/1960s 'Nouvelle Vague', or 'New Wave', movement inherited a cinema that didn't speak for them at all. So in its place they erected a new one: brash, youthful and brimming with ideas. Perhaps the most iconoclastic among them was Jean-Luc Godard.

Born in Switzerland, but settling in Paris, Godard discovered film in the capital's underground cine clubs. He made friends with fellow directors François Truffaut and Eric Rohmer, became a critic for the influential *Cahiers du Cinéma* magazine, and began to work on a run of films, from *Breathless* (1960) up to *Weekend* (1967), as writer-director. Godard was a pioneer and these works redefined the boundaries of the cinematic medium.

The story of a young Parisian hood (Jean-Paul Belmondo), *Breathless* was shot on the fly with a lightweight camera, so it feels like real life – not constructed or restricted – and exemplified many of the Nouvelle Vague's tics and tricks. Long tracking shots, such as the eight-minute effort in *Weekend*, follow the characters' freewheeling lives and were often shot from a wheelchair. Disorienting jump cuts were introduced to cut running times, but have the effect of finessing the action into smaller, significant-seeming moments. Meanwhile, references to (chiefly American) cinema history abound: Belmondo knowingly channels Bogart in *Breathless*, the futuristic

## FILMS TO SEE
★ *Breathless* (1960)
★ *Contempt* (1963)
★ *Alphaville* (1965)
★ *Masculine, Feminine* (1966)
★ *Weekend* (1967)

## DID YOU KNOW?
In 2010 Godard was awarded an honorary Academy Award for services to the cinema but, characteristically, did not attend the ceremony.

Cinema is the most beautiful
fraud in the world.

 JEAN-LUC GODARD

*Alphaville* (1965) is in thrall to film noir, and the self-reflexive *Contempt* (1963) is a film about film-making. But Godard tackled weightier subjects, too. *The Little Soldier* (1963) looks at torture in the Algerian War of Independence; *Masculine, Feminine* (1966) examined the politics of youth culture; while *La Chinoise* (1967) foresees the student revolutions of 1968. Soon he had renounced 'commercial' cinema altogether, forming a left-wing collective for obscure efforts such as *Tout va bien* (1972).

From *Passion* (1982) to *Goodbye to Language* (2014), Godard has edged back towards the mainstream, but he has never lost his anger or his experimentalism – *Goodbye*, for example, was filmed in 3D. In the words of Orson Welles: 'What's so admirable about him is his marvellous contempt for the machinery of movies and even movies themselves – a kind of anarchistic, nihilistic contempt for the medium – which, when he's at his best and most vigorous, is very exciting.' Perhaps that's why he allows his characters stare straight into the camera, as if daring us to feel the same. ★

*Contempt*, 1963

*Breathless*, 1960

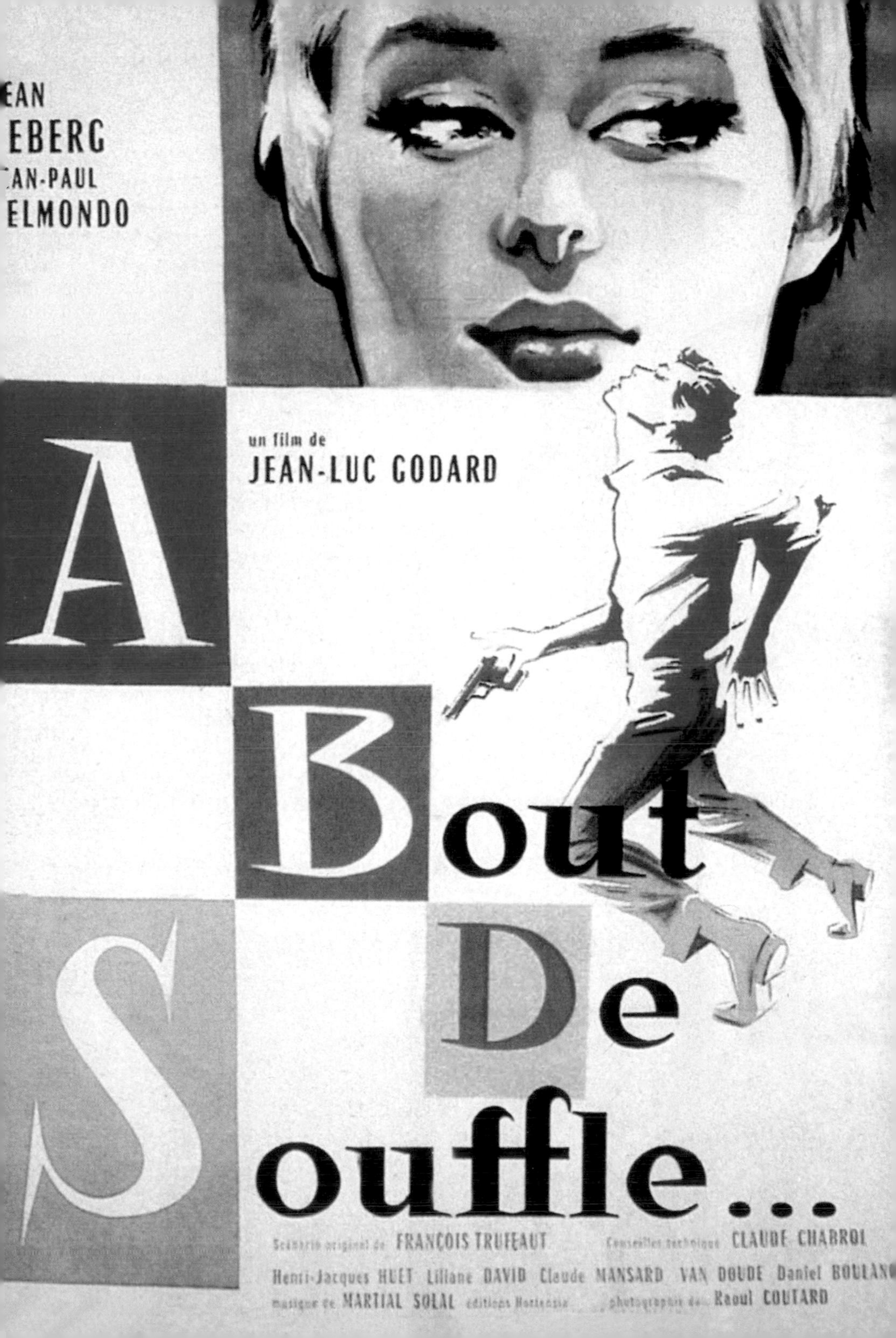
EAN
EBERG
EAN-PAUL
ELMONDO
un film de
JEAN-LUC GODARD
A
Bout
De
Souffle...
Scénario original de FRANÇOIS TRUFFAUT
Conseiller technique CLAUDE CHABROL
Henri-Jacques HUET Liliane DAVID Claude MANSARD VAN DOUDE Daniel BOULAN
musique de MARTIAL SOLAL éditions Hortensia
photographie de Raoul COUTARD

# WERNER
# **H**ERZOG

GERMAN

BORN 1942

Of the writer-directors who emerged from the New German Cinema of the 1970s, Munich-born Werner Herzog Stipeti is the most prolific, consistent and eccentric. Mixing fiction and documentary into strange, new forms, he used non-actors such as ex-mental patient Bruno Schleinstein, star of historical drama *The Enigma of Kaspar Hauser* (1974), to tell scarcely credible true stories. For example, the escape of Vietnam POW Dieter Dengler inspired the documentary *Little Dieter Needs to Fly* (1997) and the drama *Rescue Dawn* (2006), starring Christian Bale.

Looking beyond the apex of human ambition, Herzog's films are often journeys into the unknown for both audience and crew. *Aguirre, Wrath of God* (1972) and *Fitzcarraldo* (1982) took the director and star Klaus Kinski into the wilds of South America to imagine the fates of real-life pioneers. Like Francis Ford Coppola's *Apocalypse Now* (1979), which they inspired, the films became documents of their own unhinged making. In *Fitzcarraldo*, Herzog really did drag a 320-ton steamboat across the Amazon Basin. During the hellish *Aguirre* shoot, Kinski threatened to shoot the director, and himself.

Throughout Herzog's career, the clash between man and nature is repeatedly restaged, with death or insanity the only possible outcomes. Documentary *Grizzly Man* (2005) re-enacted the grisly fate of a delusional bear tracker; *Nosferatu* (1979) pits its

## FILMS TO SEE

★ *Aguirre, Wrath of God* (1972)
★ *The Enigma of Kaspar Hauser* (1974)
★ *Nosferatu the Vampyre* (1979)
★ *Fitzcarraldo* (1982)
★ *Grizzly Man* (2005)

## DID YOU KNOW?

At the end of the arduous *Even Dwarfs Started Small* (1970) shoot, Herzog threw himself into a cactus patch to appease the actors. 'Getting out was a bit more difficult than jumping in,' he explained.

I believe the common denominator of the universe is not harmony, but chaos, hostility, and murder.

 *GRIZZLY MAN*

victims against bats, rats and the eponymous bloodsucker (Kinski, again); while the opening shot of *Aguirre* – a seemingly endless procession of Spanish soldiers trekking down through the clouds into the jungle, armour, sedan chairs and all – is the history of human folly in little.

Life, for Herzog, is a ceaseless series of existential traps, hence the swirling river rapids of *Aguirre*, *Fitzcarraldo* and *Nosferatu the Vampyre*, or the chicken cursed to dance in circles at the climax of *Stroszek* (1977). It is only fitting, then, that he should revisit the same themes. Besides, as critic Roger Ebert said, 'Even his failures are spectacular.' ★

*Fitzcarraldo*, 1982

*Nosferatu the Vampyre*, 1979

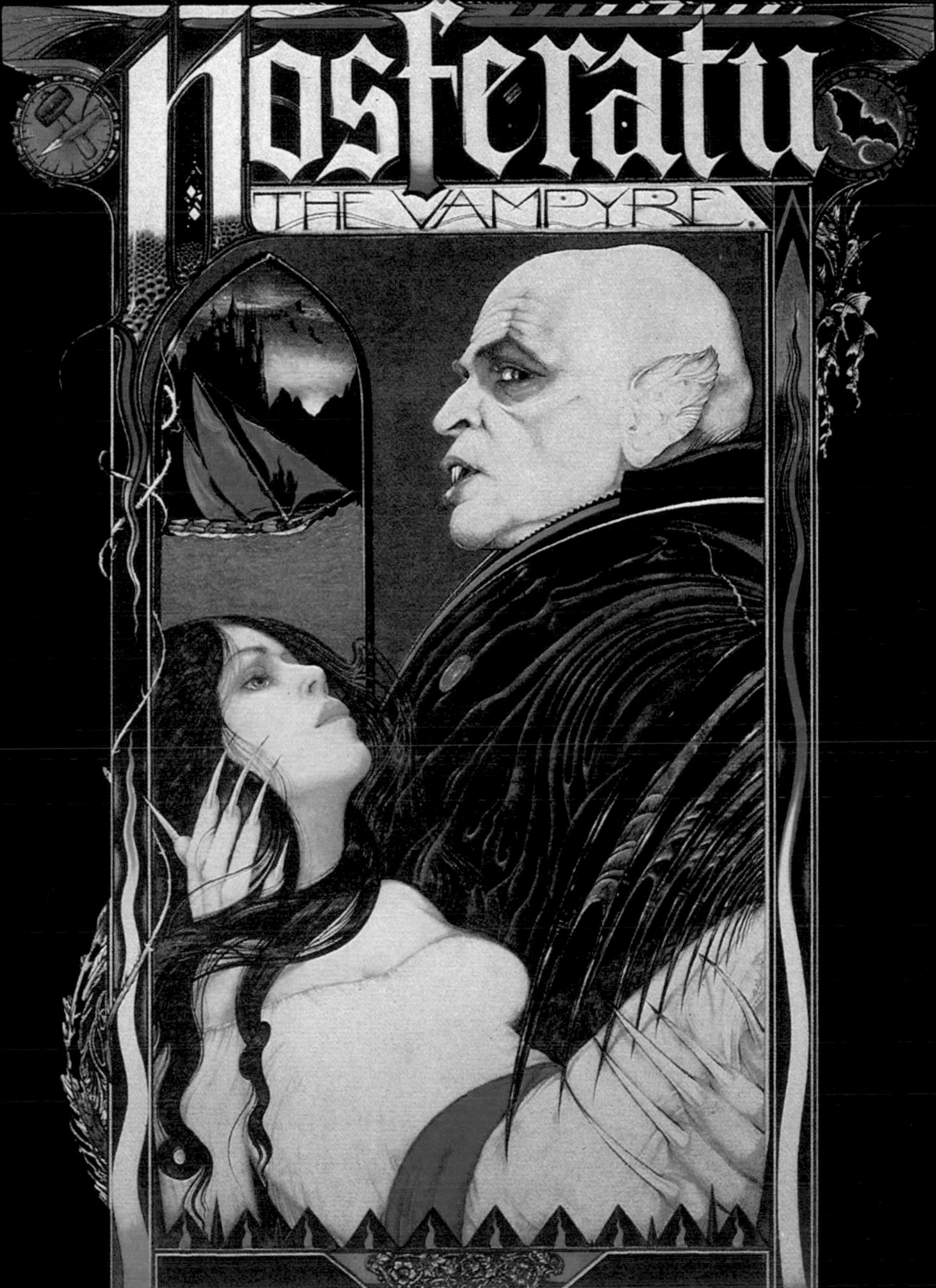
Nosferatu
THE VAMPYRE

# ALFRED **H**ITCHCOCK

BRITISH
1899–1980

Perhaps the only director recognizable from just an outline (the silhouetted squiggle he drew for fans that graced his *Alfred Hitchcock Presents* TV show), 'Hitch' stamped his signature across some of the greatest suspense films ever made. Born at the end of the Victorian era, the son of a Leytonstone grocer, he served a thorough apprenticeship at several London studios, graduating from title-card designer to scriptwriter to the director's chair for 1922's ill-fated (and unfinished) *Number 13*. But it was *The Lodger* (1927) that set the template: a foggy thriller of shifting suspicions, it starred Ivor Novello as a man who may or may not be a Jack the Ripper-style killer. The director himself considered it the first true 'Hitchcock' picture, and spent the rest of his career wittily refining what that meant, first in England, then in Hollywood.

What it meant was precisely shot – and exhaustively storyboarded – 'frightmares' based around chases (*The 39 Steps*, 1935), murders (*Rear Window*, 1954) and psychological anomalies (*Vertigo*, 1958). It meant dapper stars such as Jimmy Stewart, icy blondes like Grace Kelly, and overbearing mothers, of which Mrs Bates (*Psycho*, 1960) surely takes the cake. But it also meant show-stopping set pieces such as the Statue of Liberty climax of *Saboteur* (1942), *Psycho*'s horrendous shower murder, jaggedly edited to scything strings, or the relentless avian attacks of *The Birds* (1962), set to an electronic soundtrack of squawking, swarming gulls. All this amid

## FILMS TO SEE

★ *Strangers on a Train* (1951)
★ *Rear Window* (1954)
★ *Vertigo* (1958)
★ *North by Northwest* (1959)
★ *Psycho* (1960)

## DID YOU KNOW?

As a child, Hitchcock was locked in a police cell as punishment for misbehaving. 'I can still hear the clanging of the jail door behind me,' he told biographer Charlotte Chandler, years later.

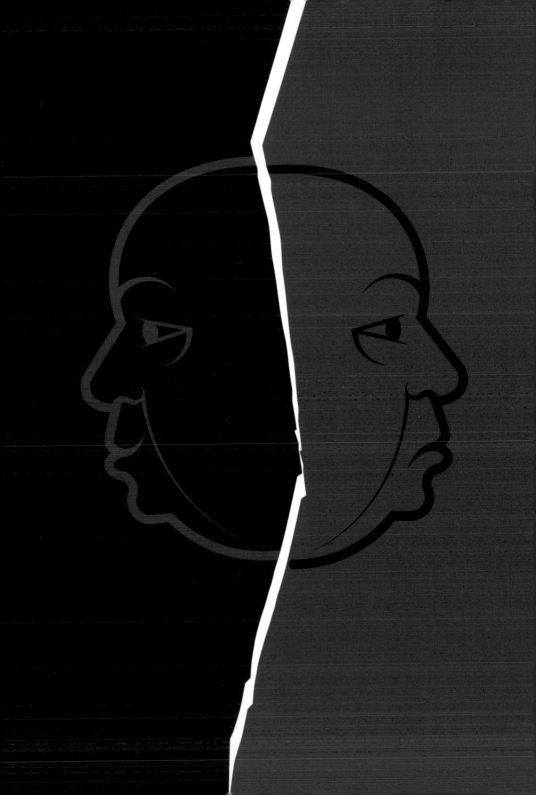

*North by Northwest,* 1959

bursts of formal experimentation: *Lifeboat* (1944) was filmed on just one set, *Rope* (1948) in ten continuous takes, *Dial M for Murder* (1954) in new-fangled 3D. These innovations kept Hitch ahead of the curve for six decades, during which he witnessed the rise and fall of the studios, the coming of sound and colour, and the death of the star system, in the process becoming one himself.

Besides memorably mischievous cameos, like *Lifeboat*'s before-and-after weight-loss advert, Hitch hosted his own trailers and TV shows, even inspiring the *Alfred Hitchcock Mystery Magazine*, which is still printed today. But it was far from empty showmanship. Between *Strangers on a Train* (1951) and *The Birds* (1963), Hitch hit a run of brilliance so singular that the adjective 'Hitchcockian' was coined. Once the highest cine-compliment, it is now just another reminder of a legacy that hangs over film history like that silhouette. ★

My theory is that everyone is a potential murderer.

 *STRANGERS ON A TRAIN*

*Vertigo, 1958*

PARAMOUNT PRESENTS

# JAMES STEWART
# KIM NOVAK
## IN ALFRED HITCHCOCK'S
## MASTERPIECE

'VERTIGO'

# ALEJANDRO GONZÁLEZ IÑÁRRITU

MEXICAN
BORN 1963

No matter where in the world he makes movies, Alejandro González Iñárritu's work has a hectic, randomly hewn rhythm that evokes Mexico City, his home town. Juggling interconnected tales of happenstance and fate, he not only keeps all the balls in the air, he does so with style to spare.

After working his way across Europe and Africa as a teenager, Iñárritu became a radio DJ – when he must have learned to balance all kinds of contrasting voices – then station director. He created his own production company and made his first feature, *Amores perros* (2000), in partnership with scriptwriter Guillermo Arriaga, who penned all of the so-called *Death Trilogy*. Beginning with a car crash, this Scorsese-esque drama about illegal dogfights showed different lives clattering together and was a critical and commercial success. *21 Grams* (2003), another look at the spiralling consequences of an accident, transplanted the action to the United States and featured big-name actors such as Sean Penn and even bigger themes such as parenthood, addiction and guilt.

*Babel* (2006) travelled further afield, setting its stories in Morocco, Mexico, the United States and Japan, across three continents and in four languages. Beginning with two young goat herders firing gunshots into the distance, it retained the sense that random violence can strike at any time, combining A-list stars such as Brad

## FILMS TO SEE
★ *Amores perros* (2000)
★ *21 Grams* (2003)
★ *Babel* (2006)
★ *Biutiful* (2010)
★ *Birdman* (2014)

## DID YOU KNOW?
Of all the critical plaudits for Iñárritu's films, the most remarkable is Javier Bardem's Academy Award nomination for *Biutiful*. It is the first time that an actor has been nominated for a role in which he speaks entirely in Spanish.

> People, they love blood.
> They love action.
> Not this talky, depressing,
> philosophical bullshit.

 *BIRDMAN*

Pitt and Cate Blanchett with non-professional actors cast along the way.

*Biutiful* (2010), Iñárritu's first solo effort, is calmer and more focused than the films he made with Arriaga. Javier Badem plays a single father struggling to scrape a living in a dowdy apartment in Barcelona, only to discover that he is suffering from terminal cancer. Praised for its melancholy poetry, the film nonetheless had some critics complaining that Iñárritu was stuck in an unrelentingly grim rut. This is to miss, however, the unexpectedly gracious ending.

*Babel*, 2006

Black comedy *Birdman* (2014), the tale of a washed-up actor (Michael Keaton) haunted by his role as a blockbuster superhero of many decades earlier, may be his most frenetic work yet. A behind-the-scenes exposé of Broadway madness, it captures the backstage chaos with a roving camera that barely ever seems to cut, so the whole thing feels – impossibly – like it is being shot live. How's that for hectic? ★

*Birdman, 2014*

# JEAN-PIERRE JEUNET

FRENCH
BORN 1953

Amélie Poulain (Audrey Tatou), the wide-eyed Montmartre waitress at the centre of Jeunet's 2001 breakthrough of the same name, loves looking back at the audience when she is at the cinema, watching their faces light up in the darkness. It is tempting to imagine the French director doing the same, because each Instagrammed frame he produces is primed to delight.

Born in Roanne, in the Loire region, Jeunet taught himself camera craft and studied animation, before co-directing a series of shorts with designer Marc Caro that were so home-made the film-makers even rolled up their sleeves to cut the negatives themselves. Together they wrote and directed darkly futuristic fantasies such as *Delicatessen* (1991), about a Sweeney Todd-alike butcher, and *The City of Lost Children* (1995), a Roald Dahl-ish tale of a dream-stealing scientist. Jeunet went solo for *Alien Resurrection* (1997), the fourth film in the increasingly beleaguered sci-fi franchise, before finding his métier with smash-hit rom-com *Amélie*, whimsical World War I drama *A Very Long Engagement* (2004), also starring Tatou alongside Jodie Foster, Looney Tunes heist movie *Micmacs* (2009) and children's adventure *The Young and Prodigious T.S. Spivet* (2013), based on Reif Larsen's cartographic novel.

But it is not Jeunet's stories that capture the imagination so much as his kid-in-a-sweet-shop stylings, all exaggerated sound effects, swooping cameras and

## FILMS TO SEE

★ *Delicatessen* (1991)
★ *The City of Lost Children* (1995)
★ *Amélie* (2001)
★ *A Very Long Engagement* (2004)
★ *The Young and Prodigious T.S. Spivet* (2013)

## DID YOU KNOW?

While filming *Engagement*, Jeunet and star Jodie Foster found themselves standing in front of Amélie's café. A tourist, not recognizing them, asked them to move so that she could get a better photograph.

*Amélie*, 2001

Failed writer, failed life...
I love the word 'fail'.
Failure is human destiny.

 *AMÉLIE*

impossible, sun-burnished vistas. It is no surprise that he had to clean up the Parisian streets to shoot the picture-perfect *Amélie* – he has an obsessive eye for tiny, telling details that accumulate to form distinctive worlds. A montage in *Delicatessen* has the residents of an apartment block variously painting the ceiling, playing the cello, pumping up a bicycle tyre and having sex at the same time, the sounds and rhythms combining to form a kinetic human symphony. Perhaps it is appropriate to think of his films as glorious Rube Goldberg machines, with disparate parts working together in eccentric, interconnected harmony to create something new. ★

*The City of Lost Children*, 1995

# KRZYSZTOF
# **K**IEŚLOWSKI

POLISH

1941–96

There is an appealing randomness to the life of Krzysztof Kieślowski that is matched in his elegantly ambling films. Born in Warsaw, but moving wherever his father, a tuberculosis sufferer, could find treatment, he trained as a fireman before switching to the arts – hardly a common career path – graduating from the Łódź Film School in 1970, after three attempts to get in.

Although his early, everyday-seeming documentaries were not pointedly political, the Polish government did not agree. TV film *Workers '71*, about the mass strikes of 1970, was heavily censored, and gradually he embraced the comparative freedom of TV dramas and features with *Personal* (1975) and *The Scar* (1976), about disillusionment in the face of oppression. But it was *The Decalogue* (1988) that announced the extent of his ambitions, a series of one-hour TV films based on the Ten Commandments. Two were released theatrically in expanded form: *A Short Film about Killing* (1988), which compares a motiveless murder with the ensuing state-sponsored execution, and *A Short Film about Love* (1988), exploring the differences, if any, between love and sex.

Based on a *Decalogue* subplot and displaying the writer-director's fondness for oddly interweaving narratives, *The Double Life of Véronique* (1991) charts the spiritual twinning between two identical but unconnected women living in Poland and France. Both are played by Irène Jacob, who has never quite been able to match her luminous

## FILMS TO SEE

★ *A Short Film about Killing* (1988)
★ *The Double Life of Véronique* (1990)
★ *Three Colours: Blue* (1993)
★ *Three Colours: White* (1994)
★ *Three Colours: Red* (1994)

## DID YOU KNOW?

Kieślowski's scripts for a final trilogy were passed to other film-makers. Tom Tykwer directed *Heaven* (2002), Danis Tanovac made *Hell* (2005), but we are still awaiting *Purgatory*.

I believe the life of every
person is worthy of scrutiny,
containing its own secrets
and dramas.

 KRZYSZTOF KIEŚLOWSKI

performance under Kieślowski's direction. For all the film's philosophical seriousness, *The Double Life* also manages to be intensely, movingly personal.

Jacob also appears in *Three Colours: Red* (1994), the final part of Kieślowski's acclaimed French–Polish *Three Colours* trilogy. Themed loosely around liberty, equality and fraternity, the French Revolutionary ideals, the trilogy's

*Three Colours: Blue*, 1993

films share characters – Juliette Binoche, star of *Three Colours: Blue* (1993), has a sneaky cameo in *Three Colours: White* (1994) and all the principals are brought together in the final climactic scene of *Red* – and each makes striking use of its eponymous hue. Moreover, they all look at the way luck, good and bad, sends our lives off at tangents, and ask whether we can really be masters of our own fates.

At the height of his success, Kieślowski did the unthinkable and announced his retirement, but the randomness wasn't over. After his death, a sculpture of two hands forming a viewfinder was stolen from his grave – surely the perfect beginning to another Kieślowski story? ★

# STANLEY
# **K**UBRICK

AMERICAN

1928–99

'If it can be written, or thought, it can be filmed,' said writer-director-producer Stanley Kubrick, who brought everything, from the dawn of man, in *2001: A Space Odyssey* (1968), to the dystopian future of *A Clockwork Orange* (1971), to the screen.

Born in the Bronx to second-generation Eastern European immigrants, Kubrick's childhood passions for chess and cameras served him well – he became a freelance photographer and began making documentaries on which he obsessively oversaw every detail. His need for control grew throughout his feature career, which began with war movie *Fear and Desire* (1953), and cycled through the genres, from film noir *The Killing* (1956) to epic *Spartacus* (1960); satire *Dr. Strangelove: Or How I Learned to Stop Worrying and Love the Bomb* (1964) to horror *The Shining* (1980); along with literary adaptations as diverse as *Lolita* (1962) and *Barry Lyndon* (1975).

Kubrick's widescreen worlds are instantly recognizable, often featuring vast new geographies that overwhelm the characters: the endless space of *2001*, or the haunted Overlook Hotel in *The Shining*. The soldiers in *Paths of Glory* (1957) and *Full Metal Jacket* (1987) lose their identities to the army, just as surely as *A Clockwork Orange*'s violent anti-hero loses his to government brainwashing. Even HAL, *2001*'s omnipotent computer, regresses to a childlike state when faced with an intelligence bigger than his own.

## FILMS TO SEE

★ *Dr. Strangelove: Or How I Learned to Stop Worrying and Love the Bomb* (1964)
★ *2001: A Space Odyssey* (1968)
★ *A Clockwork Orange* (1971)
★ *Barry Lyndon* (1975)
★ *The Shining* (1980)

## DID YOU KNOW?

Kubrick disliked flying – or Hollywood – so much that he recreated Vietnam in the London Docklands for *Full Metal Jacket* and Greenwich Village at Pinewood for *Eyes Wide Shut*.

*A Clockwork Orange*, 1971

Gentlemen, you can't fight in here, this is the War Room!

*DR. STRANGELOVE: OR
HOW I LEARNED TO STOP
WORRYING AND LOVE
THE BOMB*

Though Kubrick's characters are forced to relinquish their control, he never was, spending years researching and perfecting each film. Having relocated to England, he had the Overlook's echoing interiors built on a Pinewood Studio soundstage, and his technical precision was constantly tested by his cinematic ambition. The *2001* match cut that leaps thousands of years into the future, from a prehistoric bone to a gracefully gliding spaceship, may be the most audacious in history. Indeed, Kubrick remained wholly in charge to the last. Having screened the final cut of troubled marital drama *Eyes Wide Shut* (1999), the longest continuous film shoot ever, he died six days later. ★

*2001: A Space Odyssey, 1968*

STANLEY KUBRICK'S

# 2001: a space odyssey

STARRING
KEIR DULLEA · GARY LOCKWOOD · STANLEY KUBRICK and ARTHUR C. CLARKE
SCREENPLAY BY

PRODUCED AND DIRECTED BY STANLEY KUBRICK · IN SUPER PANAVISION® · METROCOLOR

G GENERAL AUDIENCES
All Ages Admitted

© 1968 METRO-GOLDWYN-MAYER Inc.      MGM      United Artists
Released thru
A Transamerica Company

# AKIRA
# **K**UROSAWA

JAPANESE
1910–98

The iconic writer-director of Japanese *jidaigeki* (period dramas) such as *Seven Samurai* (1954), Kurosawa may be the most homaged film-maker of all time. His *Yojimbo* (1961) birthed *A Fistful of Dollars* (1964); *The Hidden Fortress* (1958) inspired George Lucas's *Star Wars* (1977); and *Seven Samurai* was remade as a Western in *The Magnificent Seven* (1960), with another version on the way. But he also magpied himself. Crime thriller *High and Low* (1963) was based on a novel by Ed McBain (the pen name of Evan Hunter, who scripted Alfred Hitchcock's *The Birds*, 1963); *Throne of Blood* (1957) on Shakespeare's *Macbeth*; *Ran* (1985) on *King Lear*; and many of his lesser works on novels by the likes of Tolstoy and Gorky.

Born in Ōimachi in the Ōmori district of Tokyo, Kurosawa worked as an assistant director for what would become the mighty Toho studio, debuting as director with the popular action film *Sanshiro Sugata* (1943). Until fellow film-maker Yasujirō Ozu intervened, it was almost banned for being 'too American', an accusation that would plague Kurosawa's early films, but was key to his international appeal. After World War II came *yakuza* (gangster) flick *Drunken Angel* (1948), starring Toshiro Mifune, who would feature in most of Kurosawa's best work, including his masterpiece *Rashomon* (1950), which made innovative use of overlapping, unreliable narrators – hence the 'Rashomon effect'.

## FILMS TO SEE
★ *Rashomon* (1950)
★ *Seven Samurai* (1954)
★ *Throne of Blood* (1957)
★ *The Hidden Fortress* (1958)
★ *Ran* (1985)

## DID YOU KNOW?
Kurosawa was given a Lifetime Achievement Academy Award in 1990 and was posthumously named Asian of the Century in the Art, Literature and Culture category by *AsianWeek* magazine in 1999.

> Being an artist means not
> having to avert one's eyes.

 AKIRA KUROSAWA

But it was *Seven Samurai*, a tale of 16th-century villagers fighting back against bandits, that became his calling card. Shot with long lenses and multiple cameras, and making use of the 'wipe' edit that proliferates in the *Star Wars* franchise, its action scenes such as the wretched, rain-soaked finale are staged with unprecedented verve and realism. Combining these techniques with widescreen cinematography, Kurosawa ensured that even modest works such as *High and Low*, half of which takes place in one location, felt fresh and exciting.

When epic *Kagemusha* (1980), executive-produced by Lucas himself, received Cannes's prestigious Palme d'Or, the gifts that Kurosawa had bestowed upon the film world finally came back to him. ★

*Seven Samurai*, 1954

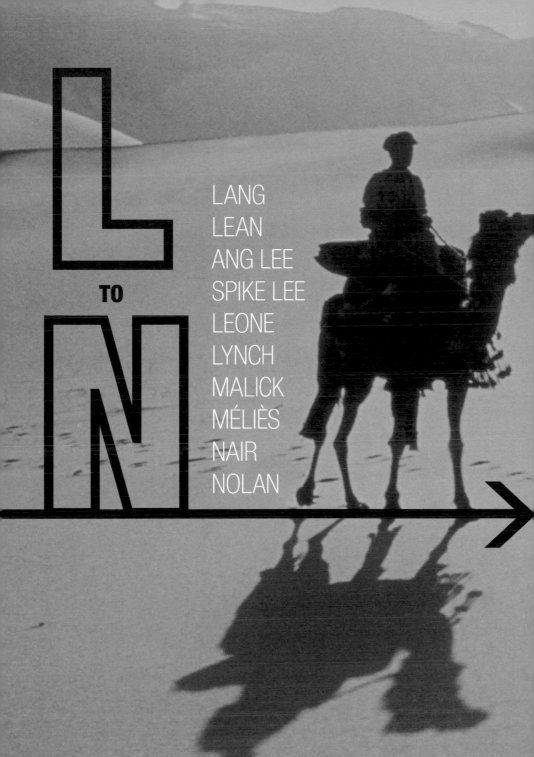

L
TO
N

LANG
LEAN
ANG LEE
SPIKE LEE
LEONE
LYNCH
MALICK
MÉLIÈS
NAIR
NOLAN

# FRITZ LANG

AUSTRIAN
1890–1976

Think of Fritz Lang, think of paranoia, pessimism and creeping dread. A product of the silent cinema, Lang wrote and directed modern genre films spiked with elements of doomy Expressionism in Germany and, later, Hollywood. Whether falsely accused, as in *Fury* (1936), on the run, as in *Hangmen Also Die!* (1943) or caught in fiendish plots spinning out of their control – Edward G Robinson's much-abused character in *Scarlet Street* (1945) is even called Chris Cross – Lang's heroes are desperate men. The opening shot of *The Testament of Dr. Mabuse* (1933), the second film in his series about a shadowy master criminal, is a sadistically slow track in on a terrified man, cowering in the corner of the villain's lair. Things go swiftly downhill for him from there.

Born in Vienna and injured during World War I, Lang moved to Berlin where he cultivated a fearsome reputation as a director (the monocle probably didn't help) and made two masterpieces. *Metropolis* (1927), the first full-length sci-fi feature, evoked a nightmarish *1984*-esque future where individual workers are lost amid vast, Brueghel-inspired sets. His first sound film, *M* (1931), is the still-chilling tale of a child murderer (Peter Lorre) terrorizing Berlin. Rumour has it that Lang pushed Lorre downstairs to add edge to the scene where he is tried by a kangaroo court of criminals. However questionable, the director's methods worked: Lorre's performance is at once terrifying and terrifyingly sympathetic.

## FILMS TO SEE
★ *Metropolis* (1927)
★ *M* (1931)
★ *The Testament of Dr. Mabuse* (1933)
★ *Fury* (1936)
★ *The Big Heat* (1953)

## DID YOU KNOW?
Lang appears as a fearsome Austrian film director, a role he was born to play, in Jean-Luc Godard's classic movie about movie-making, *Contempt* (1962).

One needs to keep closer watch over our children. All of you!

 *M*

Throughout his career Lang was wary of mobs, as well he might be. The rise of the Nazis forced him to flee to America, where he contributed minor classics such as *The Big Heat* (1953), *While the City Sleeps* (1956) and *Beyond a Reasonable Doubt* (1956) to the film noir canon – surely the most paranoid of all genres. After World War II, he returned to Berlin to make *The 1000 Eyes of Dr. Mabuse* (1960). It proved a painfully ironic title – Lang went blind soon after and never made another film. ★

*The Big Heat*, 1953

# DAVID
# LEAN

BRITISH
1908–91

For a director famous for the sprawl and scope of his films – he made 16 features in 42 years, many of them clocking in at over three hours – it is ironic that David Lean began his career as an editor.

Perhaps his love of images stemmed from his grey Croydon childhood, during which his uncle gave him a Brownie box camera; or the nights he spent at London cinemas, dreaming of escape. Working as a chartered accountant, and desperate for excitement, Lean offered his services to Gaumont-British Picture Corporation – at first for free – where he rose from tea boy to editor, cutting features by Powell and Pressburger, among others. He collaborated with Noël Coward on the war film *In Which We Serve* (1942), shooting the famous Dunkirk sequence, and made Coward's *This Happy Breed* (1944), *Blithe Spirit* (1945) and *Brief Encounter* (1945) as writer-director. Peerless adaptations of Dickens's *Great Expectations* (1946) and *Oliver Twist* (1948) followed; before *The Passionate Friends* (1949) took him to the Alps, and *Summertime* (1955) to Venice. He never looked back.

As the British film industry dwindled, Lean was hired to direct prestige international co-production *The Bridge on the River Kwai* (1957) in Sri Lanka. A fictionalized account of the building of the Burma Railway by Japanese POWs, the 161-minute epic was scarcely less daunting an undertaking itself. A celebration of the life of T E Lawrence

## FILMS TO SEE
★ *Brief Encounter* (1945)
★ *Great Expectations* (1946)
★ *The Bridge on the River Kwai* (1957)
★ *Lawrence of Arabia* (1962)
★ *Doctor Zhivago* (1965)

## DID YOU KNOW?
The 482mm lens used to film Omar Sharif riding though the desert heat haze in *Lawrence of Arabia* is known by cinematographers as the 'David Lean lens'.

starring Peter O'Toole, *Lawrence of Arabia* (1962) was even more ambitious, requiring an 18-month shoot across Jordan, Morocco and Spain. Lean stayed in Spain to recreate revolutionary Moscow for *Doctor Zhivago* (1965), another enormous hit. But the epic was drifting out of fashion. After disappointing World War I melodrama *Ryan's Daughter* (1970) and a number of unfinished projects, E M Forster adaptation *A Passage to India* (1984) proved Lean's cinematic swansong.

I like making films about characters I'd like to have dinner with.

  DAVID LEAN

Though the films got bigger and bigger, Lean never lost his editor's eye for tiny revelatory moments such as Lawrence's lit match trick, quoted in *Prometheus* (2012). Perhaps his most enduring film in this respect is *Brief Encounter*, a tale of illicit romance between married middle-aged suburbanites. Here, against the backdrop of a parochial railway station, Lean manages to convey a lifetime of sublimated feelings with the simple squeeze of a shoulder. ★

*Brief Encounter*, 1945

*Doctor Zhivago*, 1965

# ANG LEE

TAIWANESE-
AMERICAN
BORN 1954

'Every movie I make. That's my hideout, the place I don't quite understand, but feel most at home.' So says self-confessed outsider Ang Lee, a man whose films move from genre to genre so often it's as if he can't bear to stay in one spot.

Born in Taiwan but transplanted to China, then America, Lee 'was never a citizen of any particular place...' he told Roger Ebert. He studied film in New York, where he worked on Spike Lee's graduate movie (although it is hard to imagine two film-makers with more different temperaments), and submitted two screenplays to a competition sponsored by the Taiwanese government. They took first and second prizes, and became his directorial debut, *Pushing Hands* (1992), and its follow-up, *The Wedding Banquet* (1993): thoughtful culture-clash dramas about Asians getting to grips with America. *Eat Drink Man Woman* (1994), set in Taipei, completed a loose thematic trilogy.

Lee's wandering muse took him to 19th-century England for Jane Austen adaptation *Sense and Sensibility* (1995), the suburbs of 1970s America for drama *The Ice Storm* (1997) and Qing Dynasty China for martial-arts epic *Crouching Tiger, Hidden Dragon* (2000). Besides the clarity with which these disparate worlds are conjured, each film dramatizes the tension between repression and self-expression. *Crouching Tiger*'s ageing lovers Michelle Yeoh and Chow Yun-Fat can't show their feelings for each other

## FILMS TO SEE

★ *Eat Drink Man Woman* (1994)
★ *Sense and Sensibility* (1995)
★ *The Ice Storm* (1997)
★ *Crouching Tiger, Hidden Dragon* (2000)
★ *Brokeback Mountain* (2005)

## DID YOU KNOW?

Cynics speculate that *Brokeback Mountain* failed to win the Best Picture Oscar because voters were put off by its characters' bisexuality. Paul Haggis's PC crime drama *Crash* won instead.

You son-of-a-whore-son bitch, I wish I knew how to quit you.

 *BROKEBACK MOUNTAIN*

– they are too proper – so they sublimate them in extraordinary, feather-light fight sequences. The hero of comic-book blockbuster *Hulk* (2003) had repression problems all of his own.

Based on a short story by Annie Proulx, *Brokeback Mountain* (2005), a tale of forbidden love between sheep herders in the 1960s American West, proved to be Lee's masterpiece – a film, like lead actor Heath Ledger, that is hoarse with unspoken feelings. It won Lee a Best Director Oscar, which he earned again for 3D adventure *Life of Pi* (2012). Professional acceptance does not come much more emphatic, but whether Lee feels at home yet is another matter. ★

*Life of Pi*, 2012

Brokeback Mountain, 2005

# SPIKE
# LEE

AMERICAN
BORN 1957

Spike Lee's work overflows with anger. Think of the simmering racial tensions in *Do the Right Thing* (1989). Or the opening of biopic *Malcolm X* (1992), which replays the beating of Rodney King by LAPD officers over the American Stars and Stripes flag. Or the sweary monologue spat out by affluent, soon-to-be-jailed drug dealer Monty Brogan (Edward Norton) in *25th Hour* (2002), which sees him curse every resident of New York, including himself. But it's righteous rage, channelled into something constructive. *Do the Right Thing*, set in Lee's beloved Brooklyn, speaks for poor African-Americans everywhere. Documentary *When the Levees Broke* (2006) accuses the US government of failing the New Orleans communities devastated by 2005's Hurricane Katrina.

Born Shelton Jackson Lee in Atlanta, Georgia, 'Spike' grew up in Brooklyn, New York, inspiring his first student film, *Last Hustle in Brooklyn* (1977), and providing the setting for debut feature *She's Gotta Have It* (1986), about the love life of an independent woman. Shot for $175,000 over two weeks, it made a big impression in a market starved of sophisticated black cinema.

Lee's third film was *Do the Right Thing*, a vibrant portrait of neighbourhood life, in which everyone has something to say, if not always the means to say it – sometimes, like Monty Brogan, they just pour out their woes straight to

## FILMS TO SEE
★ *She's Gotta Have It* (1986)
★ *Do the Right Thing* (1989)
★ *Malcolm X* (1992)
★ *Summer of Sam* (1999)
★ *25th Hour* (2002)

## DID YOU KNOW?
Lee has clashed with most of the Hollywood firmament, joking that NRA president Charlton Heston should be shot, and berating Clint Eastwood for the lack of black soldiers in his World War II drama *Flags of Our Fathers* (2006).

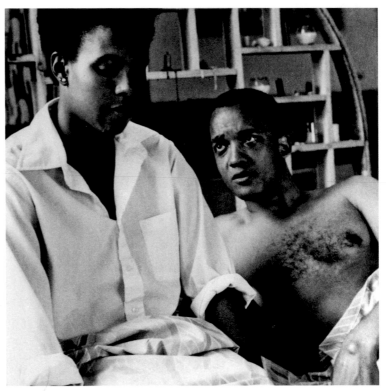

*She's Gotta Have It*, 1986

You're a New Yorker, that won't ever change. You got New York in your bones.

 *25th HOUR*

camera. The eponymous orator in *Malcolm X*, played by Denzel Washington (with Lee co-starring, as usual), had no such trouble, and the film confirmed its writer-director as one of America's most incendiary talents. Since then he has tended to juggle personal projects such as 1970s memoir *Summer of Sam* (1999) and conventional thrillers like *Inside Man* (2006) with documentaries on controversial figures such as *Mike Tyson: Undisputed Truth* (2013).

Lee may have joined the mainstream, but he hasn't given up the battle. In 2014 he recut *Do the Right Thing*'s climactic police showdown with real footage of the NYPD violently subduing Eric Garner, who later died in custody. It is proof, if proof were needed, that there is still much to be angry about. ★

*Do the Right Thing*, 1989

It's the hottest day of the summer.
You can do nothing,
you can do something,
or you can...

Bed Stuy

DO THE
Right
Thing

A
SPIKE LEE
JOINT

SAL's Famous Pizzeria

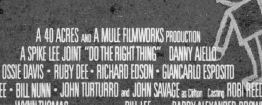

A 40 ACRES and A MULE FILMWORKS PRODUCTION
A SPIKE LEE JOINT "DO THE RIGHT THING" DANNY AIELLO
OSSIE DAVIS · RUBY DEE · RICHARD EDSON · GIANCARLO ESPOSITO
SPIKE LEE · BILL NUNN · JOHN TURTURRO and JOHN SAVAGE as Clifton   Casting ROBI REED
Production Design WYNN THOMAS   Original Music Score BILL LEE   Editor BARRY ALEXANDER BROWN
Photographed by ERNEST DICKERSON   Line Producer JON KILIK   Co-Producer MONTY ROSS   Produced, Written and Directed by SPIKE LEE
A UNIVERSAL RELEASE   SOUNDTRACK AVAILABLE ON MOTOWN RECORDS, CASSETTES AND CD'S

IVERSAL®

CIC
VIDEO

# SERGIO LEONE

ITALIAN
1929–89

Very few film-makers can claim to have founded their very own genres, but Italian writer-director Sergio Leone became the undisputed father of the spaghetti Western when he adapted Akira Kurosawa's *Yojimbo* (1961) into *A Fistful of Dollars* (1964); the dusty plains of Almeria, Spain, standing in for America's Old West, and violent realism destroying Hollywood's cosy cowboy myths.

Born in Rome to director Vincenzo Leone (billed as Roberto Roberti) and actress Edvige Valcarenghi, Leone left school to follow in his father's footsteps, becoming an assistant to neorealist auteur Vittoria De Sica on his seminal drama *Bicycle Thieves* (1948). Next, he joined the crews of American epics such as *Ben-Hur* (1959), which were shot at Rome's Cinecittà Studios, before stepping into the director's chair for sword-and-sandals flicks such as *The Last Days of Pompeii* (1959) and *The Colossus of Rhodes* (1961). The success of *Fistful* led to *For a Few Dollars More* (1965) and *The Good, the Bad and the Ugly* (1966), which Quentin Tarantino called 'the best-directed film of all time'. They became known as *The Man with No Name* trilogy thanks to Clint Eastwood's impassive avenger.

Leone heroes tended towards the taciturn – after all, men of few words are much easier to dub – plus it is hard to speak with a cheroot clamped between your teeth. He filmed them in leering close-ups or distant long shots, caught in Mexican stand-offs

## FILMS TO SEE
★ *A Fistful of Dollars* (1964)
★ *For a Few Dollars More* (1965)
★ *The Good, the Bad and the Ugly* (1966)
★ *Once Upon a Time in the West* (1968)
★ *Once Upon a Time in America* (1984)

## DID YOU KNOW?
Leone wanted younger directors such as Peter Bogdanovich and John Milius to direct his later films, with him producing. But he always ended up calling the shots himself.

There's two kinds of people... those with loaded guns and those who dig. You dig.

*THE GOOD, THE BAD AND THE UGLY*

with grizzled villains as Ennio Morricone's iconic scores filled the spaces between gunshots. *Once Upon a Time in the West* (1968) was the start of a second trilogy followed by the lesser-known comedy *Duck, You Sucker!* (1971) and completed by *Once Upon a Time in America* (1984). For his sepia-tinged swansong, Leone swapped lone gunmen for Jewish gangsters, frustrated that he had turned down *The Godfather* (1972) in the early 1970s. Truth is, he had already made enough classics for one career. ★

*Once Upon a Time in America*, 1984

*For A Few Dollars More, 1965*

# DAVID
# **L**YNCH

AMERICAN
BORN 1946

No one makes dreams into movies like David Lynch, the oddball auteur behind *Eraserhead* (1977), *Blue Velvet* (1986) and the *Twin Peaks* TV series (1990–1, with a prequel film – *Twin Peaks: Fire Walk With Me* – released in 1992). Medical drama *The Elephant Man* (1980), based on the life of sideshow act Joseph Merrick, begins with reveries of stampeding elephants. Fractured Hollywood noir *Mulholland Drive* (2001) features a recurring nightmare about a soot-faced bogeyman lurking behind a diner. Indeed, along with thematic twins *Lost Highway* (1997) and *Inland Empire* (2006), the latter may be entirely fantasy. Only Lynch knows – and he is not telling.

Born in Missoula, Montana, he travelled across the United States and Europe as a youth, before settling in Philadelphia, where he studied painting, producing canvases as strange and alluring as his films. He describes living in the dilapidated Fairmount area as 'the biggest influence in my whole life', the sense of urban paranoia seeping into lysergic shorts such as *The Alphabet* (1968), which was set to the sound of a baby crying (actually Lynch's daughter Jennifer, now a horror-film director in her own right).

Soon after, he moved to Los Angeles and made *Eraserhead*, a hypnagogic horror based on his own paternal fears. Its cult success led to the Oscar-nominated *Elephant Man*, which contrasts the surrealities of circus life – all bearded ladies and foetuses in jars – with the austerity of Victorian England. Having turned down *Return of the*

## FILMS TO SEE
★ *Eraserhead* (1977)
★ *The Elephant Man* (1980)
★ *Blue Velvet* (1986)
★ *Twin Peaks: Fire Walk with Me* (1992)
★ *Mulholland Drive* (2001)

## DID YOU KNOW?
Russian leader Mikhail Gorbachev was so keen to know the identity of the *Twin Peaks* killer that he asked President Bush to find out for him. Lynch's response when pressed? 'I can't tell you.'

This whole world's wild at heart and weird on top.

 *WILD AT HEART*

*Jedi* (1983), a director–film combination that beggars belief, Lynch made the disastrous sci-fi *Dune* (1984), based on the Frank Herbert's epic novel. But it was the twisted murder mysteries of *Blue Velvet* and *Twin Peaks* that brought him international renown.

Both starred Kyle MacLachlan as a straitlaced hero forced to look behind the veil of normality, and both followed him down the rabbit hole into danger. *Twin Peaks* unpeeled the veneers of small-town America to reveal incest, insanity and demons of the mind. In *Blue Velvet*, bland suburbia hides all sorts of psychosexual violence, the soundtrack making haunting use of Roy Orbison's 'In Dreams'. Although Lynch has since diversified into books on (what else?) transcendental meditation, and music, such as the aptly named indie collaboration *Dark Night of the Soul* (2009), his return to *Twin Peaks* in 2016 means that the nightmare is far from over. ★

*The Elephant Man*, 1980

*Blue Velvet*, 1986

# TERRENCE
# **M**ALICK

AMERICAN
BORN 1943

There are few film-makers as enigmatic as Terrence Malick. An American writer-director who disappeared off the map for 20 years in the middle of his career, he is rarely photographed, and almost never interviewed, yet he has managed to thrive while keeping Hollywood at a distance.

Raised in rural Illinois, Texas and Oklahoma, the son of a geologist, Malick studied philosophy at Harvard and Oxford, then film in California. He worked as a freelance journalist, then a script doctor, even writing an early draft of *Dirty Harry* (1971), a film not known for its philosophical musings. When road movie *Deadhead Miles* (1973), adapted from one of his screenplays, failed to gain a theatrical release, he made dreamy, lovers-on-the-run drama *Badlands* (1973) as an independent feature. Based on real crimes, it rejected doomy romanticism to introduce Martin Sheen and Sissy Spacek's dangerously dissociated teen killers, the beauty of the South Dakota scenery in stark contrast to the banality of their crimes. *Days of Heaven* (1978), a love triangle set among the farmhands of turn-of-the-century Texas, stepped further from the mainstream with its experimental editing and narration, but its luminous magic-hour cinematography remains entrancing.

After two decades of unfinished projects, Malick returned triumphant with *The Thin Red Line* (1998), less a war film than an art film shot in the midst of the Guadalcanal

## FILMS TO SEE
★ *Badlands* (1973)
★ *Days of Heaven* (1978)
★ *The Thin Red Line* (1998)
★ *The New World* (2005)
★ *The Tree of Life* (2011)

## DID YOU KNOW?
Malick is famous for editing out entire performances. Jessica Chastain, Rachel Weisz and Barry Pepper were all cut from *To the Wonder*, while Gary Oldman, Viggo Mortensen and Mickey Rourke were chopped from *The Thin Red Line*.

*Days of Heaven*, 1978

Help each other. Love everyone. Every leaf. Every ray of light. Forgive.

 *THE TREE OF LIFE*

Campaign. *The New World* (2005), a retelling of the Pocahontas story, followed in (comparatively) quick succession, with both works examining man's fragile place in the universe, each endlessly re-edited and re-tooled by Malick. But it was *The Tree of Life* (2011) that would prove his masterpiece, tackling personal demons on a spiritual plane. Inspired by the apparent suicide of his brother, Larry, in 1968, it was part coming-of-age movie, part cosmic tone poem, at one point spinning back to the beginning of time as if to ask the deities, why did this happen? Shot without a screenplay or lights, woozy romance *To the Wonder* (2012) was just as gorgeous, if a little harder to pin down, although its moniker serves as a ready-made biography title for anyone brave enough to try and get to the heart of the mystery man himself. ★

*The Tree of Life*, 2011

# GEORGES MÉLIÈS

FRENCH
1861–1938

When the Lumière brothers unveiled the *cinématographe* (an early film camera/projector, first patented by Léon Bouly in 1892) on 28 December 1895, one audience member was so spellbound he offered to buy it for 10,000 francs. The brothers turned him down, but that did not stop Georges Méliès from becoming the great 'cinemagician' of the silent age, writing, directing, photographing and starring in some 500 films.

Born Marie-Georges-Jean Méliès in Paris, young Georges grew up fascinated by stage conjurers. Working in his father's boot factory, he saved enough money to buy the Theatre Robert Houdin in 1888, where he performed magic tricks and directed shows. He made his own camera/projector, the Kinètographe Robert-Houdin, and began shooting and exhibiting one-reel shorts. Where silent cinema had been preoccupied with realism, Méliès used it to show the impossible.

Pioneering techniques such as the split screen, dissolves, time-lapse photography and the double exposure (where two images are superimposed), he delighted audiences with trick films such as *The Four Troublesome Heads* (1898), in which he appears to duet with a chorus of his own disembodied heads. Shot in black and white, but hand-painted in charmingly childish hues, *A Trip to the Moon* (1902) saw Méliès and chums chartering a rocket into space, where they frolicked with aliens played by

## FILMS TO SEE
★ *The Haunted Castle* (1896)
★ *The Four Troublesome Heads* (1898)
★ *A Trip to the Moon* (1902)
★ *The Impossible Voyage* (1904)
★ *Humanity through the Ages* (1908)

## DID YOU KNOW?
During World War I, the French army confiscated many of Méliès's prints, melting the celluloid down to make – of all things – boots.

Folies Bergère acrobats; *The Impossible Voyage* (1904), meanwhile, channelled Jules Verne on a jaunt to the sun, among other places.

Selling his wares around the world, Méliès built his own facility at Montreuil, just outside Paris, becoming, in effect, a one-man studio. He made every kind of film, from horror pictures such as *The Haunted Castle* (1896) to nudies like *After the Ball* (1897); religious offerings such as *Joan of Arc* (1900) to epics like *Humanity through the Ages* (1908), as well as adaptations of *Hamlet*, *Faust* and other out-of-copyright

*A Trip to the Moon*, 1902

texts. The list, like the magic of the films themselves, is near endless. By 1913, when he was forced to abandon his career, he had made an estimated 520 of them.

Public tastes changed, and Méliès fell out of favour. He was declared bankrupt, the theatre was sold, and he burned the negatives of his films, the sets and the costumes. After years in the wilderness – working as a toys salesman on Paris's Montparnasse railway station – Méliès's contribution to cinema was finally acknowledged in 1931 when he was presented with France's highest decoration, the Legion of Honour, by none other than Louis Lumière himself. ★

Laugh, my friends.
Laugh with me, laugh
for me, because I dream
your dreams.

 GEORGES MÉLIÈS

# MIRA
# **N**AIR

INDIAN
BORN 1957

A true citizen of the world, having lived in India, the United States and Uganda, Mira Nair makes films that are vibrant, realistic and – most importantly – humane. Born in a remote village in Orissa, India, Nair studied in Delhi, before winning a theatre scholarship to Harvard, where she discovered documentaries. She turned her film camera on the bustling byways around a Delhi mosque for documentary *Jama Masjid Street Journal* (1979), and followed a young Indian man from the Subcontinent to New York for *So Far from India* (1983).

Her feature films tread similar territory. Debut drama *Salaam Bombay!* (1988) utilized documentary techniques such as non-professional actors and location shooting to show the lives of Bombay street children, earning that exclamation mark with its giddy *joie de vivre*. The multi-award-winning *Monsoon Wedding* (2001), meanwhile, takes us behind the scenes at an arranged Punjabi Hindu wedding in Delhi, dramatizing the clashes of culture and caste with a touch as light as lens flare.

Often, her work investigates the immigrant experience in its myriad forms. *The Namesake* (2006) looks at the lives of West Bengalis in New York. *The Reluctant Fundamentalist* (2012) asks what it means to be a Pakistani man abroad in the paranoid, post-9/11 world. Even *Vanity Fair* (2004), based on the classic novel by William Makepeace Thackeray (an English novelist born in Calcutta), brought India

## FILMS TO SEE
★ *Salaam Bombay!* (1988)
★ *Monsoon Wedding* (2001)
★ *Vanity Fair* (2004)
★ *The Namesake* (2006)
★ *The Reluctant Fundamentalist* (2012)

## DID YOU KNOW?
Nair rejected an offer to direct *Harry Potter and the Order of the Phoenix* (2007), telling *Screen* magazine, 'I am better suited to emotions, human beings, and less interested in special effects.'

*Monsoon Wedding*, 2001

These are my children,
and I will protect them from
myself even, if I have to.

  *MONSOON WEDDING*

to 19th-century England with its Bollywood-inspired dance numbers. 'I recognized myself in her,' Nair told the BBC of *Vanity Fair*'s headstrong heroine Becky Sharp (Reese Witherspoon). 'I recognized all the ladies who did not want to be ladies, who wanted to buck the system that they were in.'

Women who buck the system recur in Nair's work – not least in *Amelia* (2009), a biopic of the first female pilot to fly solo across the Atlantic. Perhaps it is because she continues to do so herself, using the proceeds from *Salaam Bombay!* to set up a charitable trust for the film's child stars and founding the Maisha Film Lab to train East African film-makers. Indeed, its motto, 'If we don't tell our own stories, no one else will,' could be her own. ★

*Salaam Bombay!* 1988

153

# CHRISTOPHER
# **N**OLAN

ENGLISH-
AMERICAN
BORN 1970

Whether they are driven men trying to save the world, or damaged ones trying to escape it, Christopher Nolan's protagonists are storytellers. Amnesia-stricken Leonard Shelby (Guy Pearce) in *Memento* (2000) can't process the past, so he makes himself the star of his own film noir. Bruce Wayne (Christian Bale) in *The Dark Knight* trilogy (2005–12) turns a family tragedy into Batman's familiar superhero arc. The magicians in *The Prestige* (2006) destroy their own lives to preserve the integrity of their illusions.

Nolan's fractured narratives remain unguessable rather than unfollowable thanks to his deft use of film grammar. *Memento* is told in reverse, so we share Shelby's confusion as he works towards horrifying self-realization. Metaphysical heist flick *Inception* (2010) dips in and out of dizzying dreamscapes, but offers us real-world 'totems' such as the spinning top used by conman Cobb (Leonardo DiCaprio). Sci-fi opus *Interstellar* (2014) sees messages sent across the dimensions via Morse code. Frankly, it might as well be Nolan out there, checking that the audience is keeping up.

Though bursting with big ideas, and even bigger money shots – witness *Inception*'s Paris-of-the-mind collapsing in on itself – Nolan's films are more personal than they first seem. Broken families proliferate, perhaps something to do with a childhood split between London and Chicago; and the characters mirror their creator's all-consuming ambition. After all, this is a writer-director who made his debut, surveillance thriller

### FILMS TO SEE
★ *Memento* (2000)
★ *The Prestige* (2006)
★ *The Dark Knight* (2008)
★ *Inception* (2010)
★ *Interstellar* (2014)

### DID YOU KNOW?
Nolan never uses second-unit directors, meaning every single frame of his films was shot by him. 'If I don't need to be directing the shots that go in the movie, why do I need to be there at all?' he explained to *The Traditionalist*.

NOLAN

The smallest seed of an idea can grow. It can grow to define or destroy you.

 *INCEPTION*

*Following* (1998), for just £6,000, then called the shots on his first Hollywood movie, the Al Pacino-led detective drama *Insomnia* (2002), a mere four years later. From *Following*'s cramped London backrooms, to *Interstellar*'s infinite space, Nolan's precision-tooled blockbusters have grown larger and more complex film by film, leaving us with fascinating questions rather than facile answers. But chief among them is always: where next? ★

*Inception*, 2010

O
TO
R

OZU
PECKINPAH
POWELL & PRESSBURGER
RAY

# YASUJIRŌ OZU

JAPANESE
1903–63

Yasujirō Ozu found magic in the mundane. Though the titles of classics such as *Tokyo Story* (1953) and *Floating Weeds* (1959) are deceptively bland, these quotidian stories are packed with home truths and hidden depths. During his career as writer-director, he made 54 films of which 33 survive, most of them all but unknown outside Japan during his lifetime.

Born in Tokyo, but sent by his father to live in quiet Matsusaka, Ozu would skip school to catch epics such as *Quo Vadis?* (1912) or *The Last Days of Pompeii* (1913). Having temped as a teacher, he joined the cinematography department of Tokyo's Shochiku studio (later home to Akira Kurosawa and Takeshi Miike) and worked his way up to director on silent period piece *Sword of Penitence* (1927) and comedies such as *I Was Born, But...* (1932). The latter, which Ozu would remake as *Good Morning* (1959), concerns sons standing up to their fathers – a theme he would return to again and again.

After the war, he began the run of quiet classics, from *Late Spring* (1949) to *An Autumn Afternoon* (1962), that made his name. Of these, the wistful *Tokyo Story*, about elderly parents visiting their busy, big-city offspring, and *Floating Weeds*, about a troupe of travelling actors stirring up old secrets in a seaside town, are the most acclaimed. While other directors endlessly gilded the lily, Ozu spent his career stripping away

## FILMS TO SEE
★ *Late Spring* (1949)
★ *Tokyo Story* (1953)
★ *Good Morning* (1959)
★ *Floating Weeds* (1959)
★ *Late Autumn* (1960)

## DID YOU KNOW?
In 1927 Ozu was called to the studio director's office for punching a canteen queue jumper. He presented his boss with a film script he had written. The rest is history.

*Late Autumn*, 1960

I have formulated my own
directing style… proceeding
without any unnecessary
imitation of others.

 YASUJIRÔ OZU

filmic artifice. He avoided shooting in sound until 1936, colour until 1958, and widescreen completely, and most of his credit sequences shared the same sackcloth backing. Mellow dramas, rather than melodramas, his films elide their most sensational events so we only hear about them from the characters, most of whom look straight at the camera and are shot from below, as if we are sitting on *tatami* mats in their homes, listening. The effect is extremely intimate, continuing to draw audiences in because it makes human beings the most important things in the frame. ★

*Tokyo Story*, 1953

# SAM PECKINPAH

AMERICAN
1925–84

'If they move, kill 'em,' says William Holden's ageing outlaw at the start of seminal Western *The Wild Bunch* (1969). It is not just the title of David Weddle's excellent biography, it is emblematic of Peckinpah's entire oeuvre – for move they certainly do, and kill 'em he most certainly did.

Peckinpah's kinetic editing style combined shots of different speeds and angles to mimic the visceral confusion of battle. Meanwhile, his capacity to depict – and, in the depths of his alcoholism, inflict – violence earned him the nickname 'Bloody Sam'. *Cross of Iron* (1977) features a penile dismemberment, *Straw Dogs* (1971) contains a devastating double rape, and what is *Bring Me the Head of Alfredo Garcia* (1974) but a stark invitation to murder? The two came shockingly together in *The Wild Bunch*'s bullet-riddled finale, where Holden and co take on an army of Mexicans, their guns, and Peckinpah's camera, sparing no one.

If Peckinpah's work seemed most at home on the range, it is because he was. Born David Samuel Peckinpah in 1925, in Fresno, California, young Sam would skip class to hone his cowboy skills on his grandfather's ranch. These and other problems with authority would reoccur throughout his life, and he was sent to join the Marines in 1943, where he saw what bullets really do to human flesh. Back home, he broke into TV as the writer then director of wipe-clean Western shows such as *Gunsmoke*.

## FILMS TO SEE
★ *Ride the High Country* (1962)
★ *The Wild Bunch* (1969)
★ *Straw Dogs* (1971)
★ *Bring Me the Head of
    Alfredo Garcia* (1974)
★ *Cross of Iron* (1977)

## DID YOU KNOW?
Stanley Kubrick was in line to direct Marlon Brando in a Peckinpah script that eventually became Brando's *One-Eyed Jacks* (1961), but the combination of three huge egos proved too combustible.

This is where I live. This is me. I will not allow violence against this house.

 *STRAW DOGS*

His first film, *The Deadly Companions* (1961), led to a falling-out with the producer. He retained more control on the melancholic *Ride the High Country* (1962), but *Major Dundee* (1965), starring Charlton Heston as a Union cavalry officer, almost derailed his career. Over-schedule and over-budget, the film was taken off him and re-edited, not for the last time.

*The Wild Bunch*, 1969

After a few years in the wilderness, Peckinpah came back with all guns blazing in *The Wild Bunch*, which pitted Holden's veteran killers against encroaching modernity. Great films, like the Cornish revenge drama *Straw Dogs*, and incomplete ones, such as the studio-butchered *Pat Garrett and Billy the Kid* (1975), followed, but the themes remained insistently the same: masculinity in crisis, the harrowing, hardening effects of violence, and an acknowledgement that nothing lasts for ever. 'It ain't like it used to be, but it'll do,' is *The Wild Bunch*'s final line, a compromise Peckinpah himself could never reach. ★

# MICHAEL | EMERIC
# **P**OWELL | **P**RESSBURGER

MICHAEL
**P**OWELL
BRITISH
1905–90

EMERIC
**P**RESSBURGER
HUNGARIAN-
BRITISH
1902–88

A burst of Technicolor brilliance amid the drab black-and-white of World War II, Michael Powell and Emeric Pressburger brought Hollywood scope and ambition to kitchen-sink Britain in films such as *The Life and Death of Colonel Blimp* (1943), *A Matter of Life and Death* (1946), *Black Narcissus* (1947), *The Red Shoes* (1948) and *The Tales of Hoffmann* (1951).

Born in Kent, and trained as a banker, director Michael Powell worked his way up through the UK's fledgling film industry, even shooting stills on Hitchcock's *Blackmail* (1929), before he helmed thriller *The Spy in Black* (1939) for producer Alexander Korda. Korda brought in fellow Hungarian émigré Imre 'Emeric' Pressburger to help, a journalist/screenwriter who had fled Nazi-era Berlin. 'I was rejoicing that I was going to be working with someone like this,' said Powell, and the two joined forces on some 20 films up to *The Boy Who Turned Yellow* (1972).

Like the Coen brothers, Powell and Pressburger collaborated so closely that the roles of scriptwriter, director and producer blurred together. They formed The Archers production company, which had the marvellous manifesto, 'We refuse to be guided or coerced by any influence but our own judgement.' That judgement was sound. Proudly English, but non-parochial, The Archers' films explored bright new worlds – the Himalayas in religious drama *Black Narcissus*; the south of France

## FILMS TO SEE
★ *The Life and Death of Colonel Blimp* (1943)
★ *A Matter of Life and Death* (1946)
★ *Black Narcissus* (1947)
★ *The Red Shoes* (1948)
★ *Peeping Tom* (Powell only; 1960)

## DID YOU KNOW?
Powell was married to film editor Thelma Schoonmaker, who helped craft some of Martin Scorsese's best works. When *Peeping Tom* received critical reappraisal later in the 20th century, Scorsese was its most outspoken fan.

We were born thousands
of miles apart, but we were
made for each other.

 *A MATTER OF LIFE AND DEATH*

in ballet extravaganza *The Red Shoes* – and huge emotions, often, literally, matters of life and death. *Colonel Blimp* pined for long-lost love; *Life and Death* replayed the horrors of war as a cosmic bureaucratic battle. Endlessly elegant and technically daring – witness the POV shots from David Niven's closing eyes in *Life and Death*'s surgical scene – their films also contained that rarest of ingredients, 'A little bit of magic...' as Pressburger put it.

The partnership dissolved in 1957, with a few lesser, later reunions. Pressburger continued writing war films such as *Operation Crossbow* (1965), while Powell made controversial *Psycho*-alike *Peeping Tom* (1960), effectively ending his own career. Neither regained the spark they found in collaboration. 'He knows what I am going to say even before I say it – maybe even before I have thought it – and that is very rare,' Emeric Pressburger once told the BBC. 'You are lucky if you meet someone like that once in your life.' ★

*A Matter of Life and Death*, 1946

*Peeping Tom*, 1960

# PEEPING TOM

EASTMAN COLOUR

# SATYAJIT
# **R**AY

INDIAN
1921–92

Indian writer-director Satyajit Ray made universal dramas that said more about his homeland than the shiny diversions of Bollywood ever could. 'Not to have seen the cinema of Satyajit Ray means existing in the world without seeing the sun or the moon,' said Japanese director Akira Kurosawa, Ray's contemporary and cohort.

Born in Calcutta, to an affluent family of poets and printers, Ray was a movie-magazine obsessive. He studied art, worked at a British-run advertising agency and was sent to London, where the films of Italian director Vittoria De Sica and France's Jean Renoir (whom Ray would assist on Renoir's India-set drama *The River*, 1951) inspired him to try independent film-making. Back home, he began shooting *Pather Panchali* (1955) using non-professional actors and his own rapidly depleting funds. Based on a classic coming-of-age novel about a rural Bengali boy called Apu (Subir Banerjee), it took three years to complete but beguiled audiences at the 1956 Cannes Film Festival, where it won the sweetly apposite award for 'Best Human Document'. Two sequels followed – *Aparajito* (1956) and *Apur Sansar* (1959) – and the *Apu Trilogy* was later voted among the greatest of all time by the very publications Ray had pored over as a child.

Ray's early international success combined with the modest budgets of his films allowed him total creative control over his work, and his prolific output – a feature nearly

## FILMS TO SEE

★ *Pather Panchali* (1955)
★ *Aparajito* (1956)
★ *Jalsaghar* (1958)
★ *Apur Sansar* (1959)
★ *Charulata* (1964)

## DID YOU KNOW?

Ray's unmade script of *The Alien* (1967) was passed around Hollywood for years. Ray believed that it inspired *E.T.* (1982), although Steven Spielberg denied any connection.

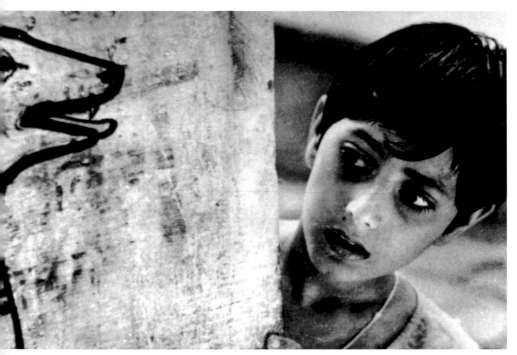

*Pather Panchali*, 1955

I am not conscious of being
a humanist. It's simply that
I am interested in human
beings.

 SATYAJIT RAY

every year until the 1980s, when he suffered his first heart attack – included everything from musical fantasy *Goopy Gyne Bagha Byne* (1969) to *Ganashatru* (1990), an adaptation of Ibsen's play *An Enemy of the People*. But it was those human documents he excelled at, most notably *Jalsaghar* (1958), which dramatizes the last days of a dying aristocrat, and a trio of films that demanded equality for Indian women: *Devi* (1960), *Mahanagar* (1963) and *Charulata* (1964). His *Calcutta Trilogy* (1970–6), meanwhile, criticized the city's endemic corruption.

In 1992, 24 days before his death, Ray became the first – and only – Indian to receive an Honorary Academy Award, calling it, the 'best achievement of [my] movie-making career'. The rest of the world, on the other hand, would find it impossible to pick just one. ★

# S

**TO**

# T

SCORSESE
SCOTT
SEMBÈNE
SPIELBERG
TARANTINO
TRUFFAUT

→

# MARTIN
# **S**CORSESE

AMERICAN
BORN 1942

As far back as Martin Scorsese can remember, he always wanted to be a film-maker. Growing up in New York's Little Italy, the young Scorsese was prevented from playing sports by severe asthma, so he fell in love with movies instead. From Ingmar Bergman to Federico Fellini, his tastes were as wide-ranging as the films he would come to make himself, leaving no genre untapped or unmastered.

After film school and the Roger Corman apprenticeship common among the 1970s 'movie brats', he began making New York tales of battered machismo and bloody redemption such as *Mean Streets* (1973), *Taxi Diver* (1976) and *Raging Bull* (1980), all three starring Robert De Niro. The 1980s brought dark laughs from *The King of Comedy* (1983) and dense literary adaptations such as *The Last Temptation of Christ* (1988); the 1990s, classic crime epics from *Goodfellas* (1990) to *Casino* (1995); while the new millennium has seen him looking back at the power struggles of the last with *Gangs of New York* (2002) and *The Wolf of Wall Street* (2014), starring new muse Leonardo DiCaprio.

The exuberance of his technique – all blaring rock 'n' roll soundtracks, jarring jump cuts and ambitious tracking shots like the famous Copacabana club walk-through in *Goodfellas* – is matched by a real sense of character. Who can forget the threatening to-the-mirror monologues of *Taxi Driver*'s Travis Bickle ('You talkin' to me?') or

## FILMS TO SEE
★ *Taxi Driver* (1976)
★ *Raging Bull* (1980)
★ *The Last Temptation of Christ* (1988)
★ *Goodfellas* (1990)
★ *The Departed* (2006)

## DID YOU KNOW?
With eight nominations, Scorsese is the most Oscar-nominated director alive, but he has taken home the Best Director award only once, for *The Departed*.

Someday a real rain will come and wash all this scum off the streets.

 *TAXI DRIVER*

*Raging Bull*'s Jake LaMotta ('I coulda been a contender...'), the latter a quote from Elia Kazan's *On the Waterfront* (1954).

Scorsese's characters love movies as much as he does. Pivotal scenes in *Taxi Driver* and double-crossing cop thriller *The Departed* (2006) take place at the pictures, while 3D children's adventure *Hugo* (2011) is an ode to a forgotten hero of silent cinema. In 1990 Scorsese founded The Film Foundation, which is 'dedicated to protecting and preserving motion-picture history'. Few would dispute that he is now an essential part of it himself. ★

*Taxi Driver*, 1976

*Raging Bull*, 1980

# RIDLEY
# **S**COTT

BRITISH
BORN 1937

Where some directors set out to make films, Ridley Scott sets out to make worlds. Think of the gothic, grimly practical habitations in pioneering sci-fi horror *Alien* (1979), or the neon skyscrapers in future noir *Blade Runner* (1982) – part Hong Kong, part hell on earth. But he also brought us replicas of the past, in sword-and-sandals revival *Gladiator* (2000); bullet-riddled Mogadishu, in war film *Black Hawk Down* (2001); and a Grimm Brothers fairyland, in *Legend* (1985). 'Building better worlds' is the motto of the *Alien* franchise's Weyland Corporation, but perhaps Scott's should be 'building worlds better'. For all the technological advancements, *Blade Runner*'s Los Angeles convinces because it is still awash in adverts and acid rain. Similarly, in *Alien*, the *Nostromo* spaceship's oil-rig chic helps ground H R Giger's glisteningly gruesome creatures.

Born in England's industrial north to an army family, Scott moved around Europe as a child – hence, perhaps, his fascination with new places. As a young man he studied at London's prestigious Royal College of Art, where he made a black-and-white short called *Boy and Bicycle* (1962), starring younger brother Tony (the late director of *Top Gun*, 1986, and *True Romance*, 1993, among others). After a stint designing for the BBC, Scott began making award-winning commercials, then graduated to features. Set during the Napoleonic era, *The Duellists* (1977) was an impressive debut, but

## FILMS TO SEE
★ *Alien* (1979)
★ *Blade Runner* (1982)
★ *Thelma & Louise* (1991)
★ *Gladiator* (2000)
★ *Matchstick Men* (2003)

## DID YOU KNOW?
*Alien* writer Dan O'Bannon had plenty of practice at being lost in space – he played Pinback in John Carpenter's *Dark Star* (1974). Pinbacker is also a character in Danny Boyle's *Sunshine* (2007).

I have seen things you people wouldn't believe. Attack ships on fire off the shoulder of Orion. I watched c-beams glitter in the dark near the Tannhäuser Gate. All those moments will be lost in time, like tears in rain. Time to die.

 *BLADE RUNNER*

it was *Alien* that kick-started his Hollywood career. Since then, the likes of feminist road movie *Thelma & Louise* (1991) and *Gladiator* have kept him relevant; and he even returned to the franchise that made his name with *Prometheus* (2012).

Whether the biblical Egypt of *Exodus: Gods and Kings* (2014) or the medieval England of *Robin Hood* (2010), Scott is as concerned with the look of his films as what happens in them. But modest efforts such as con flick *Matchstick Men* (2003) and cop thriller *American Gangster* (2007) put their human dramas ahead of their designs and, besides, there is a good reason for the multiple cuts (there are seven versions of *Blade Runner*, of which five are available on DVD) and unruly running times – he doesn't want to leave. ★

*Alien*, 1979

*Blade Runner*, 1982

# OUSMANE
# **S**EMBÈNE

SENEGALESE
1923–2007

Dubbed the 'father of African film', Ousmane Sembène made a stand against corruption, colonialism and pernicious tribal traditions, both in his life and in his work.

The son of a fisherman, Sembène was born in Ziguinchor, in the former French colony of Senegal. He dropped out of school as a teenager, served in the Free French Army during World War II and, on his return, participated in the Dakar–Niger railroad strike (1947–8) to win African workers the same rights as the French. With few prospects in Senegal, he stowed away on a ship bound for France, and worked as a longshoreman in Marseilles, becoming an active trade unionist. The injustices he saw inspired his first novel, *The Black Docker* (1956), but his breakthrough book, *God's Bits of Wood* (1960), harked back to his railroad days, and his focus returned to Africa.

Although he continued to write novels, some of which he adapted for the screen, when Sembène returned to Dakar after a year studying cinema in Moscow, he started a pioneering film career. *Borom Sarret* (1963), a short about an impoverished cart driver, was the first film shot in Africa by a black African. Feature debut *Black Girl* (1966), which centred on a Senegalese servant mistreated by her French masters, was the first black African film shown at Cannes, where it won the Prix Jean Vigo. *Mandabi* (1968), meanwhile, about the chaos and greed caused by a windfall, swapped French for the West African Wolof language. World War II-era dramas *Emitaï* (1971) and

## FILMS TO SEE

★ *Black Girl* (1966)
★ *Mandabi* (1968)
★ *Xala* (1975)
★ *Camp de Thiaroye* (1988)
★ *Moolaadé* (2004)

## DID YOU KNOW?

Sembène frequently toured his films around Senegal and held audience debates after screenings. He felt that the villagers often understood his films better than the critics did.

*Moolaadé*, 2004

At a moral level, I don't think
we have anything to learn
from Europe.

 OUSMANE SEMBÈNE

*Camp de Thiaroye* (1988) continued this trend, but were suppressed for criticizing the colonial government.

'I create to talk to my people, my country,' Sembène told the *Independent*. 'Africa needs to see its own reflection. A society progresses by asking questions of itself, so I want to be an artist who questions his people.' To this end, he satirized the Senegalese government by comparing it to an impotent businessman in *Xala* (1975), while *Faat Kiné* (2000) and *Moolaadé* (2004) decried the treatment of women in African culture. The latter, another Cannes winner, was a plaintive plea against the horrors of female genital mutilation (FGM). It proved both his masterpiece and his swansong. ★

Grove Press
International
Film Festival
SENEGAL-FRANCE

# MANDABI

A Grove Press International Film Festival Presentation
A Film by Ousmane Sembene—Produced by Jean Maumy
A Domireve (Dakar) and C.F.F.P. (Paris) Film

# STEVEN
# **S**PIELBERG

AMERICAN
BORN 1946

When 27-year-old wunderkind Steven Spielberg made *Jaws* (1975), a film nearly sunk by its star, a malfunctioning mechanical shark, he (accidentally) invented the summer blockbuster. He has been accused of infantilizing audiences ever since. While no stranger to childish pleasures – *Jurassic Park* (1993) pauses to marvel at its own CG dinosaurs, and the *Indiana Jones* films (1981–2008) present an exotic past of unkillable heroes and dastardly Nazis – his best work engenders a sense of childlike wonder in viewers.

Born in Cincinnati, Ohio, but raised in small-town New Jersey and Arizona, the young Spielberg borrowed his father's movie camera to make a Western for his Scouts' photography merit badge (as a self-referential link, Indiana Jones is shown as a boy scout in *The Last Crusade*, 1989). As a teenager he shot his own mini epics, splitting his time between Arizona and Saratoga, California, when his parents divorced. While working as an unpaid intern for Universal Studios, he directed the 26-minute, hippy-ish *Amblin'* (1968), which led to feature-length TV film *Duel* (1971) – essentially *Jaws* on wheels – and his big-screen debut, lovers-on-the-run drama *Sugarland Express* (1974). The unprecedented success of *Jaws*, coupled with sci-fi *Close Encounters of the Third Kind* (1977) and Indie's first outing, *Raiders of the Lost Ark* (1981), gave Spielberg the keys to the kingdom. Since then he has become one

## FILMS TO SEE

★ *Jaws* (1975)
★ *Indiana Jones and the Raiders of the Lost Ark* (1981)
★ *E.T.* (1982)
★ *Schindler's List* (1993)
★ *Saving Private Ryan* (1998)

## DID YOU KNOW?

In 1982 Spielberg spent $60,500 to buy a certain prop from Orson Welles's *Citizen Kane* (1941). If you've seen the film, you will know *exactly* which one it is.

When I grow up, I still want
to be a director.

 STEVEN SPIELBERG

of the most successful directors of all time, repeating his key themes like the five-note refrain in *Close Encounters*.

Damaged families and absent fathers recur in everything from *Hook* (1991) to *Minority Report* (2002). Slavery, racism and the fragile foundations of the United States are explored in *The Color Purple* (1985), *Amistad* (1997) and *Lincoln* (2012). The horrors of war are brought to brutal, thudding life in *Saving Private Ryan* (1998) and *Empire of the Sun* (1987), the latter seen through the eyes of a child; while black-and-white Holocaust drama *Schindler's List* (1993) used a solitary little-girl-lost in a red coat to make us mourn the millions dead. Far from childish, these are films about the end of innocence. Even *E.T.* (1982), a life-affirming tale of a boy who befriends an alien, acknowledges the darkness of the adult world. Its most famous image – and the logo of Spielberg's Amblin Entertainment – is the heroes bicycling across the sky, but it is the moon, not the sun, that lights their way. ★

*Schlindler's List*, 1993

*E.T.*, 1982

# QUENTIN
# TARANTINO

AMERICAN
BORN 1963

Appropriately enough, it was a motor-mouthed video-store clerk who became the king of American indie cinema. Working at Los Angeles's now-defunct Video Archives, Tarantino would champion unloved genre films to customers. Not short of chutzpah, he decided he could do better, and did.

Born in Knoxville, Tennessee, the young Tarantino moved to California, where his mother's boyfriends would take him to blaxploitation films. He took acting classes and wrote savvy screenplays, one of which would become his directorial debut, *Reservoir Dogs* (1992), a Hong Kong action cinema-inspired heist-gone-wrong flick filled with profane, postmodern dialogue and graphic, ear-slicing violence. It was followed by *True Romance* (1993) and *Natural Born Killers* (1994), commercial, controversial movies based on his scripts, and sprawling, self-referential (and, indeed, self-reverential) gangster opus *Pulp Fiction* (1994), which won the Palme d'Or and a Best Screenwriting Oscar. But more interesting work was to follow these eye-catching first salvoes.

*Jackie Brown* (1997), an adaptation of Elmore Leonard's 1992 novel *Rum Punch*, starred 1970s legend Pam Grier, and suggested Tarantino might actually care for his characters as well as mouthing along with them. *Kill Bill: Vol. I & Vol. II* (2003 & 2004), a samurai-inflected revenge saga split in two, showcased dazzling set pieces as much

## FILMS TO SEE
★ *Reservoir Dogs* (1992)
★ *Pulp Fiction* (1994)
★ *Jackie Brown* (1997)
★ *Kill Bill: Vol. I & Vol. II* (2003 & 2004)
★ *Inglourious Basterds* (2009)

## DID YOU KNOW?
Mia Wallace, Uma Thurman's character in *Pulp Fiction*, sketches out the plot of *Kill Bill* nine years early when she describes the *Fox Force Five* pilot she appeared in.

*Reservoir Dogs*, 1992

All you can do is pray for a quick death, which you ain't gonna get.

 *RESERVOIR DOGS*

as the director's DVD collection and features a heart-rending performance from muse Uma Thurman. *Inglourious Basterds* (2009) rewrote World War II as a *Dirty Dozen*-style caper without shying away from the horrors perpetrated by the SS. Similarly, the slavery-themed *Django Unchained* (2013) mixed spaghetti-Western violence with blaxploitation sass, winning Tarantino his second Screenwriting Oscar. He threatens to retire after his next Western, *The Hateful Eight* (2015).

Whether resurrecting the careers of forgotten actors such as Harvey Keitel (*Reservoir Dogs*), John Travolta (*Pulp Fiction*) and David Carradine (*Kill Bill*), or pilfering the titles/plots of forgotten films such as *Django* (1966), *City on Fire* (1987) and *Lady Snowblood* (1973), Tarantino has always paid his dues to the past. In 2007 he bought Los Angeles's New Beverley Cinema, where he programmes lost classics alongside his own films, as if walking the Video Archives aisles anew. ★

*Pulp Fiction*, 1994

# FRANÇOIS TRUFFAUT

FRENCH
1932–84

Lots of critics become film-makers, but few succeed after so profoundly poisoning their own well. As a reviewer for *Cahiers du Cinéma*, Truffaut was dubbed 'the gravedigger of French cinema', so it was only right that he should be the one to resurrect it. Truffaut's life was steeped in film, but it was also an actual life – he had experienced reform school, the army and prison before he ever wielded a camera.

Growing up in Paris, Truffaut never knew his father and was side-lined by his mother's new husband. He escaped to the cinema and, when excluded from school, decided to teach himself by watching three films a day and reading three books a week. He started his own film club, the Cercle cinémane ('the Movie Mania Club'), in 1948, and was sent to reform school for stealing a typewriter to fund it. He befriended *Cahiers* editor André Bazin, joined the army, and was sent to prison for desertion. Upon release he began writing – voraciously – about the subject he loved best. With contemporaries Jean-Luc Godard, Claude Chabrol and Eric Rohmer, he founded the French Nouvelle Vague, the 'New Wave' of cine-literate *auteurs*: a *Cahiers* term devised by Truffaut that made writer-directors like himself the authors of their own personal visions.

What makes Truffaut's personal visions so compelling is the interplay between autobiography and allusion. *The 400 Blows* (1959) homaged Jean Vigo's *Zero for*

## FILMS TO SEE
★ *The 400 Blows* (1959)
★ *Jules and Jim* (1962)
★ *Fahrenheit 451* (1966)
★ *Day for Night* (1973)
★ *The Last Metro* (1980)

## DID YOU KNOW?
Steven Spielberg gave Truffaut a pivotal acting role in *Close Encounters of the Third Kind* (1977). No typewriters were stolen.

I have always preferred the reflection of the life to life itself.

 FRANÇOIS TRUFFAUT

*Conduct* (1933) to tell the tale of Antoine Doinel (Jean-Pierre Léaud), a 13-year-old sent to reform school for stealing – guess what? – a typewriter. It won Truffaut the Best Director prize at Cannes, a festival from which he had been banned as a journalist, and he revisited Doinel's story in semi-autobiographical efforts *Stolen Kisses* (1968), *Bed and Board* (1970) and *Love on the Run* (1979). Elsewhere, *Shoot the Piano Player* (1960) was a cut-up love letter to American gangster films; *Jules and Jim* (1962), a freewheeling *ménage à trois*; *Fahrenheit 451* (1966), a *1984*-inflected ode to bibliophilia. Later works such as *Day for Night* (1973), a film about film-making, and *The Last Metro* (1980), a celebration of culture during the German occupation, ensured his critical standing among the next generation of cineastes.

'The film of tomorrow will not be directed by civil servants of the camera, but by artists for whom shooting a film constitutes a wonderful and thrilling adventure,' he wrote in 1958, before embarking on some wonderful, thrilling adventures of his own. ★

*Jules and Jim,* 1962

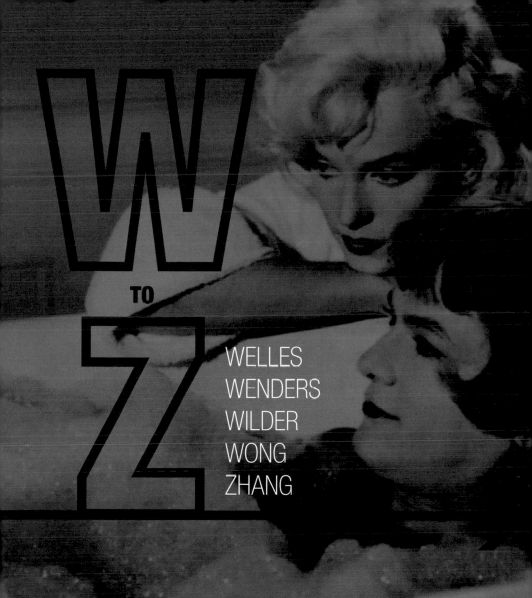

# W to Z

WELLES
WENDERS
WILDER
WONG
ZHANG

# ORSON
# **W**ELLES

AMERICAN
1915–85

An actor-writer-director-producer of the airwaves, stage and screen, Welles may be the greatest 'multi-hyphenate' of all time, but his name is also a byword for wasted potential. In his topsy-turvy career he made just 13 full-length films, many of them re-edited by other hands, or scuppered by his own. Consider the quality-chasm between his first, *Citizen Kane* (1941), in which he played a world-famous tycoon, and his last, *The Transformers: The Movie* (an animated children's film directed by Nelson Shin, and also the last role of actor Scatman Crowthers; 1986), in which he voiced a planet-eating robot.

Born in Kenosha, Wisconsin, Welles had an itinerant upbringing. His mother died when he was nine, his father when he was 15, and his brother was institutionalized. Somehow from the chaos he forged a career in theatre and radio. In just four years he was responsible for a triumphant *Julius Caesar* (1937) on Broadway; a controversial radio adaptation of H G Wells's *The War of the Worlds* (1938), which fooled listeners into thinking aliens had really invaded; and *Kane*, often considered the greatest film of all time.

With *Citizen Kane*, the 25-year-old director created an astonishing edifice to the possibilities of cinema. Dizzy with technique (including flashbacks, montages, temporal cuts), it featured extraordinary deep-focus photography and a daringly

## FILMS TO SEE
★ *Citizen Kane* (1941)
★ *The Magnificent Ambersons* (1942)
★ *Othello* (1952)
★ *Touch of Evil* (1958)
★ *Chimes at Midnight* (1965)

## DID YOU KNOW?
As a young man visiting Ireland, Welles walked into Dublin's Gate Theatre and proclaimed himself a Broadway star. Nobody believed him, but he got a part all the same.

Mr Kane was a man who
got everything he wanted
and then lost it.

 *CITIZEN KANE*

non-linear narrative. Unfortunately, it was clearly based on the life of newspaper magnate William Randolph Hearst, who subsequently did all he could to ruin Welles's career. Not that Welles needed much help, leaving a trail of unrealized projects such as an adaptation of Joseph Conrad's *Heart of Darkness* (which would later underpin Francis Ford Coppola's *Apocalypse Now*, 1979) and *Don Quixote* (later attempted by the equally disaster-prone Terry Gilliam).

Of the films he did complete, dynastic drama *The Magnificent Ambersons* (1942) was beautifully shot and acted but badly recut by the studio; *Othello* (1952) took three years to film, and longer to get a US release; Mexico-set noir *Touch of Evil* (1958) featured some of the most virtuoso tracking shots ever committed to celluloid; while *Chimes at Midnight* (1965) saw him playing another flawed man-mountain, Shakespearean *bon viveur* Falstaff. But it is *Kane* to which we always return, a story of shooting for the moon and missing. Kane, we are told, 'lived to be history' but 'outlived his power to make it'. The same could be said for Welles himself. ★

*Touch of Evil*, 1958

*Citizen Kane*, 1941

# WIM
# **W**ENDERS

GERMAN
BORN 1945

'The camera', said writer-director Wim Wenders, 'is a weapon against the tragedy of things, against their disappearing.' To this end, his early experiments such as *Silver City* (1969) – which is made up of static shots of urban landscapes – were records as much as stories, and his best work is steeped in sad remembrance.

Born in Düsseldorf with Dutch heritage, Wenders studied medicine and philosophy at university, before dropping out, running away to Paris and working as an engraver – another weapon against things disappearing. During this time, he immersed himself in cinema, returning to Germany to study film and become a critic. His feature debut, *Summer in the City* (1970), was an aimless wander through West Germany, and his filmography is full of stories and journeys that go, ostensibly, nowhere such as *The Goalkeeper's Fear of the Penalty* (1972), which features a motiveless murder the narrative does not even begin to solve.

A trilogy of German-set road movies followed, beginning with *Alice in the Cities* (1974); the last of them, *Kings of the Road* (1976), stated that, 'The Americans have colonized our subconscious.' They certainly colonized Wenders's. Neo-noir *The American Friend* (1977) took novelist Patricia Highsmith's all-American psychopath Tom Ripley (the anti-hero of five books beginning with *The Talented Mr. Ripley*, 1955, filmed in 1999) to Hamburg; *Hammett* (1982) was a fictionalized account of the crime

## FILMS TO SEE
★ *The American Friend* (1977)
★ *Paris, Texas* (1984)
★ *Wings of Desire* (1987)
★ *Buena Vista Social Club* (1999)
★ *Pina* (2011)

## DID YOU KNOW?
A talented photographer, Wenders shot a series of landscapes from Australia to Japan for his long-running series *Pictures from the Surface of the Earth*.

A lot can happen to a man
in four years, I guess.

*PARIS, TEXAS*

writer's San Francisco adventures; while heart-sick drama *Paris, Texas* (1984), whose very title suggests Europe transplanted to the United States, has an aggressively red-white-and-blue colour scheme.

Whether the immutable Texas desert or the ever-changing Berlin of *Wings of Desire* (1987), landscapes play an integral role in Wenders's work, much of which deals with painful pasts. The guardian angel in *Wings* watches over a city still scarred by World War II, while Harry Dean Stanton's lost soul in *Paris, Texas* has been rendered all but mute by trauma, a silent tragedy etched forever on his face. Wenders's American friend Ry Cooder, who provided *Paris, Texas* with its lovely, lonely slide guitar score, would become the unlikely star of *Buena Vista Social Club* (1999), a celebration of Cuban music that, like 3D dance extravaganza *Pina* (2011), exhibits an altogether more joyful side to Wenders's work. Perhaps it is because, as documentaries, they represent tragedies averted. ★

*Paris, Texas,* 1984

*Pina,* 2011

# BILLY
# **WI**LDER

AUSTRIAN-
AMERICAN
1906–2002

Billy Wilder's characters can't half talk. Whether anxious voiceover or rat-tat-tat repartee, these busy, brassy city types never stop analyzing, pitching and kvetching. Legendary film noir *Double Indemnity* (1944) has salesman Fred MacMurray confessing his own sorry tale of murder and betrayal by Dictaphone; caustic corporate rom-com *The Apartment* (1960) begins with a splurge of facts and figures from Jack Lemmon's worrisome insurance clerk.

Born Samuel Wilder in the former Austro-Hungary, 'Billy' (as his mother called him) studied journalism and moved to Berlin, where he broke into movies as a screenwriter, a role he satirized in Hollywood drama *Sunset Boulevard* (1950) – 'Words, words, more words!' complains faded star Gloria Swanson to scribe William Holden – but one he excelled at, winning three of his six Oscars for his incisive, effusive scripts.

Like so many German-based Jews, Wilder fled during Hitler's rise to power, settling first in Paris, where he made the forgotten drama *Bad Seed* (1934), then Hollywood. Here, he co-wrote screwball comedy *Ninotchka* (1939) for fellow émigré director Ernst Lubitsch, before tackling both roles on the Ginger Rogers vehicle *The Major and the Minor* (1942). Over 50 years, and 60 films, Wilder showed himself to be one of the greats, as adept at witty dramas as he was at chatty comedies. *The Lost Weekend* (1945) plumbed the lowest depths of alcoholism; *Sunset Boulevard* poked fun at

## FILMS TO SEE

★ *Double Indemnity* (1944)
★ *The Lost Weekend* (1945)
★ *Sunset Boulevard* (1950)
★ *Some Like It Hot* (1959)
★ *The Apartment* (1960)

## DID YOU KNOW?

After winning the Best Picture Oscar for *The Artist* (2011), French director Michel Hazanavicius said: 'I would like to thank the following three people, I would like to thank Billy Wilder, I would like to thank Billy Wilder, and I would like to thank Billy Wilder.'

*Double Indemnity*, 1944

All right, Mr DeMille, I'm
ready for my close-up.

 *SUNSET BOULEVARD*

Tinseltown's corrosive self-obsession. Even farces such as *The Seven Year Itch* (1955) and cross-dressing classic *Some Like It Hot* (1959), both starring Marilyn Monroe, had their cynical sides; the precarious balance between light and dark proving key to their enduring appeal.

Watched today, Wilder's films still seem impossibly fresh. Snappily paced (see *Double Indemnity*'s breakneck beginning), risqué (*Some Like It Hot*'s censor-baiting sexual politics), and possessing a wickedly postmodern sense of humour (*Sunset Boulevard*'s knowing cameos from silent star Buster Keaton, among others), they also contain some of cinema's most cherishable performances, with 14 of his stars earning Oscar nominations. Wilder passed on in 2002 and was buried in the same cemetery as Monroe. In reference to *Some Like It Hot*'s iconic last line, one obituary read: 'Billy Wilder dies. Nobody's perfect.' He wasn't far off. ★

*Some Like It Hot*, 1959

# **W**ONG KAR-WAI

CHINESE
BORN 1958

To distinguish – and perhaps distance – themselves from the movies of Mainland China, Hong Kong's New Wave directors of the 1970s and 1980s worked in Cantonese rather than Mandarin, shooting on location amid the rush-and-push of their beloved city. The most distinguished among them is Wong Kar-wai, whose sensuous art films such as *Chungking Express* (1994), *Happy Together* (1997), *In the Mood for Love* (2000) and *2046* (2004) are filled with longing.

Born in Shanghai, but moving to Hong Kong in 1963 – where he did not, at first, speak the language – Wong took comfort in the cinema. He studied graphic design, became a scriptwriter, and made his directorial debut with crime melodrama *As Tears Go By* (1988). It was a hit, but over time he developed the more personal style evinced in 1960s-set drama *Days of Being Wild* (1990).

Whether fleeting (*Chungking Express*), unrequited (*In the Mood for Love*) or illicit (*Happy Together*), his films explore doomed romance in all its forms. Often, it blooms between strangers, the random nature of metropolitan life throwing them together before pulling them apart again just as quickly.

Suffused with a woozy, late-night melancholy, *Chungking Express* spins lovelorn stories from chance backstreet meetings; *In the Mood for Love*, meanwhile, tells of a chaste affair between two apartment-block neighbours. Even in these mundane

## FILMS TO SEE
★ *Chungking Express* (1994)
★ *Happy Together* (1997)
★ *In the Mood for Love* (2000)
★ *2046* (2004)
★ *The Grandmaster* (2013)

## DID YOU KNOW?
To persuade Tony Leung to play a homosexual character in *Happy Together*, Wong Kar-wai presented him with a fake script, which was dumped on the first day of filming.

settings, Wong manages to bring a sense of lushness. *Happy Together*'s recurring image is the vibrant colours and violent motion of a waterfall, providing a stark contrast with the scratchy, black-and-white boredom of the central couple, two gay men arguing their way round South America. Often, as here, he ignores the script completely, assembling his films from a patchwork of stolen moments.

Perhaps his most beautiful work to date, *The Grandmaster* (2013) brings depths of unspoken emotion to the humble martial-arts flick. As Tony Leung and Zhang Ziyi indulge in gravity-defying fisticuffs, and the image shimmers into slow motion, it feels more like foreplay than fighting. Trust him to make a kung fu film that is more *Brief Encounter* (1939) than Bruce Lee. ★

I never want to make beautiful pictures. I just want to make sure it's right.

 WONG KAR-WAI

*2046*, 2004

*In the Mood for Love*, 2000

# ZHANG YIMOU

CHINESE
BORN 1951

Mainland China's best-known director makes epic films about individual struggles – something he understands all too well. Born in Xi'an, north-western China, Zhang left school to work as a labourer during the political upheaval of the Cultural Revolution (1966–76). He took up painting and photography, then, when the Beijing Film Academy reopened in 1978, petitioned to enter despite being too old and completely without experience.

The quality of his photographs secured him a place and, after graduating, he worked as a cinematographer and actor, before making his directorial debut with *Red Sorghum* (1987), a characteristically lush look at the difficulties of rural life starring then-partner Gong Li, who would grace many of his films right up to *Coming Home* (2014). Technicolor period drama *Ju Dou* (1990) was the first Chinese release to be nominated for an Academy Award for Best Foreign Language Film, and *Raise the Red Lantern* (1991) the second. Dramas such as *To Live* (1994) courted controversy with the government for depicting the hardships endured by ordinary Chinese people, but continued to win Zhang praise – and prizes – internationally.

After Ang Lee's *Crouching Tiger, Hidden Dragon* (2000) ignited the world's interest in *wuxia* (martial arts) films, Zhang hit back with *Hero* (2002), *House of Flying Daggers* (2004) and *Curse of the Golden Flower* (2006): vividly coloured and choreographed

## FILMS TO SEE
★ *Red Sorghum* (1987)
★ *Raise the Red Lantern* (1991)
★ *Hero* (2002)
★ *House of Flying Daggers* (2004)
★ *Curse of the Golden Flower* (2006)

## DID YOU KNOW?
Zhang's early work criticized the Chinese government – a brave move – but *Hero* was deemed to go too far the other way. In protest, he withdrew the film from the 1999 Cannes Film Festival.

Because of the influence
of Chinese martial arts films,
Hollywood movies
are changing.

 ZHANG YIMOU

dramas that looked to the past for their conflicts. What is so striking about these movies isn't just the gorgeous hues – each of the flashbacks in *Hero* is colour-coded for clarity, and the noble folk of *House* and *Curse* stroll the rainbow corridors of impossibly opulent palaces – but the director's wondrous feel for movement.

*Hero*, 2002

*Hero* sees Tony Leung and Jet Li levitating across a misty lake; *Curse* features black-clothed attackers swooping through a narrow gorge like bats; while *House*'s narrative stops in its tracks to witness Zhang Ziyi's blind assassin dance, her flowing robes defying gravity. It is no surprise that the director was asked to oversee the opening/closing ceremonies of the 2008 Beijing Summer Olympic Games.

Many years in the making, Zhang's next project is his most ambitious yet, an international co-production about the building of the Great Wall of China – perhaps the ultimate example of humankind turning adversity into something incredible. ★

# GLOSSARY

**auteur** (Fr. 'author') Term used to describe a film director with a creative vision distinct and personal enough that – despite the collaborative nature of film-making – it is reflected strongly in each film and, indeed, their entire body of work. The notion was first developed in the 1950s by François Truffaut, for whom this kind of 'authored' film was an ideal to be aspired to (if, as he later admitted, impossible to achieve). From the 1960s onwards the idea has been much criticized, principally because it undervalues the contribution of other participants in the film-making process (screenwriters, cinematographers, actors etc).

**B-movie** A low-budget commercial film, often belonging to the Western, horror or science-fiction genres.

***Cahiers du Cinéma*** A French film magazine founded in 1951 that became closely associated with the directors of the Nouvelle Vague such as Jean-Luc Godard, François Truffaut and Eric Rohmer, who all contributed articles. The magazine was a proponent of auteur cinema. Since the 1950s it has undergone considerable evolution but still retains a certain influence today.

**film noir** (Fr. 'black film') Term retrospectively used to describe the black-and-white crime films made by Hollywood throughout the 1940s and 1950s. These were often based on the hardboiled detective fiction of the 1930s and appropriated the cinematic techniques of German Expressionism such as the dramatic use of light and shadow. Whether film noir ever constituted a distinct genre is a matter of critical debate.

***giallo*** (It. 'yellow') A largely Italian genre that is part whodunnit, part slasher, and named after a series of lurid mystery novels with yellow covers.

**Hays Code** Properly called the Motion Picture Production Code, Hollywood's strict moral guidelines were introduced by the Motion Picture Producers and Distributors of America (MPPDA) in 1930 and took their name from MPPDA president Will H Hays. By the late 1950s the code was only nominally enforced and was finally abandoned in 1968.

***jidaigeki*** A Japanese genre of period dramas, often showing the adventures of samurai (caste warriors) and following an established set of dramatic conventions.

**neo-noir** Term loosely applied to post-1970 films that consciously take up and rework the conventions of the classic film noirs of the 1940s and 1950s, often in contemporary settings. A notable example is the German film *The American Friend* (dir. Wim Wenders, 1977).

**neorealism** An Italian movement of the 1940s and 1950s. The term describes films that were often shot on location, employing non-professional actors and addressing working-class themes. *Rome, Open City* (dir. Roberto Rossellini, 1945) is often considered the quintessential neorealist film.

**New German Cinema** Term used to describe a generation of German film-makers from the 1960s and 1970s who took inspiration from the French Nouvelle Vague. Notable directors who at least started in this mode include Rainer Werner Fassbinder, Werner Herzog and Wim Wenders. The movement brought about a renaissance in German film-making after the long period of stagnation that followed the Nazi period.

**New Hollywood** Often referred to as the 'American New Wave', New Hollywood applies to the period in American cinema stretching from the late 1960s to the mid-1970s during which films became less studio-led and more director-led – that is, stamped with the personal vision of the director (*see* auteur). New Hollywood films typically had a strong countercultural feel, were often stylistically experimental and appealed to a younger, college-educated audience. The seminal example of New Hollywood cinema is *Bonnie and Clyde* (dir. Arthur Penn, 1967).

**New Wave** *See* Nouvelle Vague.

**noir** *See* film noir.

**Nouvelle Vague** (Fr. 'New Wave') Term applied to a generation of French film-makers, including Jean-Luc Godard, François Truffaut, Claude Chabrol, Jacques Rivette and Eric Rohmer, whose work was characterized by an increased spontaneity and freedom, key techniques such as the jump cut and long takes, and an engagement with the political and cultural upheavals of the period (such as the May 1968 student uprising).

**Panaglide** *See* Steadicam.

**point of view (POV)** A shot showing what a particular character sees. The effect is most pronounced in horror films such as *Halloween* (dir. John Carpenter, 1978), where the camera mimics the movements and eyeline of an (unseen) character, encouraging the audience to identify with them.

**special effects (SFX)** Visual or sound effects introduced into a film either on set (e.g. the use of prosthetics or a snow machine), 'in camera' (e.g. multiple exposure or coloured filters) or during post-production (e.g. dissolves and slow motion). Since the 1990s the development of CGI (computer-generated imagery) has revolutionized the production of special effects.

**split screen** The visible division of the film screen into two or more parts, showing multiple scenes. The device can be used *inter alia* to show simultaneous events, draw ironic contrasts or disrupt the viewer's illusion of reality.

**Steadicam** A device, introduced in 1975, that enables a camera to be strapped to the operator's body, absorbing the inevitable shakes and jerks associated with handheld cinematography, and ensuring smooth, gliding shots. The device brought a new fluidity and freedom to film-making.

**stop motion** Animation technique by which an object or character is repeatedly filmed while tiny adjustments are made to its stance or appearance between frames, thereby creating the illusion that it is moving of its own accord.

**storyboard** A method of pre-visualizing a motion picture by presenting the story as a sequence of graphic images. The technique was first developed for animation at Walt Disney Productions during the early 1930s.

**Super 8** A film format released by Eastman Kodak in 1968 for the home-movie market but used by some independent film-makers who fetishize its intimate documentary feel.

**Technicolor** A colour motion picture process first invented in 1916 and dominating Hollywood film-making from the 1920s to the early 1950s. Filming using Technicolor produced saturated, hyper-real colours and was often favoured in musicals and costume dramas. Most famously, the colour scenes in *The Wizard of Oz* (1939) exploit its dazzling effects.

**tracking shot** A shot in which the camera is mounted on a wheeled platform (known as a 'dolly') that is pushed along rails while a scene is filmed.

**Western** Genre of film especially popular in early and classical Hollywood, focusing on stories set in the American West of the late 19th century and after. Often Westerns depict the conflicts between European settlers and Native Americans, usually from the former's point of view. More recent, 'revisionist' Westerns challenge the racist and/or sexist stereotypes of the genre's heyday.

**widescreen** Strictly applied to any film image with a width-to-height aspect ratio greater than the standard 1.37:1 Academy aspect ratio provided by 35mm film. The widescreen ratio was brought in to differentiate cinema from TV and is traditionally used to emphasize its spectacular aspects, as in today's IMAX film releases.

# INDEX

# PICTURE CREDITS —

# ACKNOWLEDGEMENTS

Like a film no book is the vision or production of just one person, there are long crew lists, key roles and unsung heroes. And so it is with this book, which could not have come into being without those mentioned below:

My gratitude goes to Matt Glasby, our equivalent screenwriter, for his insight and knowledge into the lives and work of each director. Our shared love of film meant we hit it off from the first production meeting and it was a joy to work together. Not forgetting, of course, the executive producer, aka my editor Hannah Knowles, for again having the vision to believe this a worthwhile project. My thanks to Pauline Bache, first AD, working hard on the ground, keeping everyone to schedule. Thanks, also, to Giulia Hetherington for finding such great photos for the book, and to Meskerem Berhane for her sterling production work. I am also grateful to Himesh Kar for his thoughts and guidance on international directors. And the Oscar goes to Olivia Wilkes, my Best Supporting Actress.

Commissioning Editor  Hannah Knowles
Editor  Pauline Bache
Creative Director  Jonathan Christie
Designer  Andy Tuohy
Picture Researcher  Giulia Hetherington
Production Controller  Meskerem Berhane